D0937094

MEN OF POWER

MEN OF POWER

VOL. I

SixTY-MINUTE BIOGRAPHIES

THOMAS JEFFERSON
CHARLES DICKENS
MATTHEW ARNOLD
LOUIS PASTEUR

By

FRED EASTMAN

Essay Index Reprint Series

 BOOKS FOR LIBRARIES PRESS
FREEPORT, NEW YORK

INTERNATIONAL STANDARD BOOK NUMBER:
0-8369-1991-2

LIBRARY OF CONGRESS CATALOG CARD NUMBER:
74-128236

PRINTED IN THE UNITED STATES OF AMERICA

FOREWORD

I shall try to *explain* these men, not expose or glorify them. They all had power. Where did they get it? They accomplished great things for the common good. Why? Together with the men in the four succeeding volumes in this series they bequeathed to us no small part of our social, scientific, political, and spiritual heritage. How? To paraphrase Shakespeare's line,

> The cause, dear reader, is not in their stars,
> But in themselves, that they were conquerors.

In these studies I hope to discover the influences that operated to lift these men above the level of the commonplace and to set their feet on higher ground. I shall present each man's heredity, his cultural and national background, his early home and school, his friendships, his purposes, his habits of work, his opponents, and his philosophy of life. From these considerations it may be possible to construct an understandable picture of his growing personality. Such biographical portraits will give more attention to each man's early struggles than to his later accomplishments, more importance to what went on within his heart as a youth and young man than to the honors that came to him as an old man.

Gratefully I acknowledge the valuable aid of three young colleagues who have helped assemble the material for these sketches—Roger Hazelton, Myron C. Settle, and Daniel Day Williams—and the constructive criticism and encouragement of my wife.

F. E.

"FROM THE LIVES OF MEN WHOSE PASSAGE IS MARKED BY A TRACE OF DURABLE LIGHT, LET US PIOUSLY GATHER UP EVERY WORD, EVERY INCIDENT LIKELY TO MAKE KNOWN THE INCENTIVES OF THEIR GREAT SOULS, FOR THE EDUCATION OF POSTERITY."

LOUIS PASTEUR.

CONTENTS

THOMAS JEFFERSON
1743-1826

IF, ON the early morning of April 13, 1743, a lantern-swinging colonial town crier had suddenly been gifted with prophecy, he might have amended his usual cry to something like this: "Two o'clock and all's well! Two o'clock and a windy morning! Born today on the Indian frontier of Albermarle County of Virginia will be Thomas Jefferson, son of Peter Jefferson and Jane Randolph Jefferson. The boy will grow up to be statesman extraordinary, scholar, linguist, architect, economist, botanist, friend of the Indian, scientific farmer. He will be founder of American democracy, author of the Declaration of Independence and of the Statute of Religious Freedom of Virginia, third President of the United States, father of the University of Virginia, prophet of social reform."

The Times. But no town crier that morning was so gifted, and the child created no more stir on that rugged frontier than any other infant. Virginia in

9

those days was the most prosperous of the English colonies. The plantations of tobacco with their slave labor provided an economic base for an aristocracy of culture, hospitality, and gaiety. Life was fair—if one belonged to the aristocracy. Young blades dressed in velvet and lace, women in billowy frocks. They drove to parties in coaches and six; they hunted, raced, sang, and dabbled in the arts. Life might have continued to be fair had not the mother country fixed an acquisitive eye upon the growing revenues of the colonists. As long as the colonies had been weak and scattered, they had been forced to depend almost entirely upon England. But now that they were growing in wealth and population their sense of dependence was decreasing. And the more England taxed them and restricted their liberties the more the colonies, though widely variant in customs, manners, industry, and background, were driven together for mutual protection.

Pregnant times! A new nation about to be born! Young Jefferson was to live through the most exciting and eventful period of American history, and one of the most eventful in European history as well. When the British treasury found itself depleted by the war with France, the famous stamp tax was passed in 1764, and fiery young Patrick Henry, a "lawyer," trained in a few weeks of reading law, flamed up in a little country church with his famous "Give me liberty or give me death" speech before the Virginia legislators who were meeting there. In 1773 came the tea tax, promptly followed by the Boston Tea Party, for the colonists objected to taxation without representation. Then came the closing of the port of Boston in 1774, and in 1775 the first General Congress passed a boycott agreement against England. In the same year "the shot heard round the world" was fired at Lexington as the embattled farmers resisted the invasion of the British redcoats. On July 4, 1776, the colonists through their representatives in the Continental Congress adopted the Declaration of Independence, and the new nation was born.

To be sure, it was a puling infant—this new nation. Five years after the adoption of the Constitution the country was still without a financial backbone, its "army" was reduced to eighty men, and its Congress was "despised abroad and disobeyed at home." But it was alive and kicking. If it could get the right mental food and nursing, it would have a future.

Thomas Jefferson took a leading part in these events. Was it by accident? Consider his parentage, his education, the classical library in his father's home, the pioneer spirit of the times, the great men with whom he came in contact, and his own self-discipline and see how they steadily shaped him for such a destiny.

His Father. Jefferson's father was a pioneer, his mother an aristocrat. His father, Peter, a man of enterprise, courage, and herculean strength, had little schooling but an eager, inquiring mind and sound judgment. A middle-class farmer, he was neither aristocrat

nor peasant. With the help of a hundred slaves he
farmed fourteen hundred acres. On winter evenings
he customarily read to his family from Shakespeare,
Swift, and Addison. He counted himself a Whig, and
his political ideas were on the liberal side. Like George
Washington, he had begun his career as a surveyor of
land. He so won the esteem of his neighbors in this
capacity that he was chosen along with Joshua Fry, professor of mathematics in William and Mary College,
"to continue the boundary line between Virginia and
North Carolina, which had been begun by Colonel
Byrd. . . ." He became Justice of the Peace and a
member of the House of Burgesses. Also as County
Colonel he was made responsible for the Indian frontier, a post of great importance to the settlers, especially after Braddock's defeat in 1755. But Peter Jefferson had the confidence of the Indians whom he treated
with justice and hospitality. His own farm, "Shadwell," lay near the Indian trail, and the chiefs used
frequently to stop with him on their way to Williamsburg, the colonial capital. There was no trouble with
the Indians while he held this post.

These Indian visitors made a strong impression on
young Thomas. Writing in 1812 to John Adams as the
two exchanged reminiscences, he said:

I knew much of the great Ontassete, the warrior
and orator of the Cherokees. He was always the guest
of my father on his journeys to and from Williamsburg. I was in his camp when he made his great fare-

well oration to his people the evening before he departed for England. The moon was in full splendour, and to her he seemed to address himself in his prayers for his own safety on the voyage and that of his people during his absence. His sounding voice, distinct articulation, animated action, and the solemn silence of his people at their several fires, filled me with awe and veneration, although I did not understand a word he uttered.[1]

Peter Jefferson determined that his eldest son, Thomas, should be a scholar, and placed him in an English school at five years of age, and in a Latin school at nine. He taught the boy self-reliance and gave him a homely precept rather rare in a slave state, "Never ask another to do what you can do for yourself." He died when Thomas was but fourteen years old, leaving to him the responsibility for Shadwell with its broad acres and splendid library of classics, and for the care of the boy's six younger sisters and younger brother and their mother.

His Mother. Thomas' mother was Jane Randolph, who had married Peter Jefferson at nineteen. There was not a family in Virginia more wealthy, proud, and influential than the Randolphs. She traced her ancestry far back to the English and Scotch squires of Warwickshire and Murray, possibly even to Queen Mary. In her blood, too, the royal Indian blood of Pocahontas

[1] Francis Hirst: *Life and Letters of Thomas Jefferson,* p. 16. This and subsequent quotations used by permission of the Macmillan Company, publishers.

was said to run. An aristocrat through and through, she bequeathed to Thomas something of her love of beauty and the arts.

Shadwell. All his life Thomas was moved by two great passions: love for his home and a desire to be of service to the great mass of common people. Those passions rooted not only in his parentage but in his early life at Shadwell. No ordinary farm, Shadwell, In the rolling Piedmont region with its valleys and wooded hills, its fields of tobacco and corn and small grain, its Negro slaves and its contact with the Indians, the great frontier farm gave the boy an opportunity for adventure and nature study he could never have had in a town. A shy, red-haired, lanky lad engaging in the sports of the day, exploring the surrounding forests, making friends with aristocrats and Indians, listening to the political talk of leading colonists around the dinner table, and to his father's reading of the classics before the fireside—something began to stir in his young heart, something which a later poet put into words:

" 'There's no sense in going further—it's the edge of
        cultivation,
    So they said, and I believed it—broke my land and
        sowed my crop—
  Built my barns and strung my fences in the little
        border station
    Tucked away below the foothills where the trails
    run out and stop.

14

Till a voice, as bad as Conscience, rang interminable
  changes
  On one everlasting Whisper day and night repeated
  —so:
'Something hidden. Go and find it. Go and look behind the Ranges—
  Something lost behind the Ranges. Lost and waiting for you. Go!' " [2]

How he escaped the prevailing vices of the youth of
that day—heavy drinking, gambling, and excessive use
of tobacco—is still something of a mystery. There was
plenty of it all around him on neighboring plantations.
Probably his father's adage: "It is the strong in body
who are also the strong and free in mind," had something to do with it. At any rate, he steered clear of
them and treasured his time and strength for more important things in the days to come.

Early Schooling. Schools were rare in the Virginia
of Jefferson's boyhood. Twenty years before his birth
the Bishop of London, of whose diocese Virginia was
a part, queried his Virginia clergy on this subject.
"Are there any schools in your parish?" he asked. All
except three of the clergymen replied, "None." "Is
there any parish library?" was his next question. Only
one answered in the affirmative, and gave a complete
inventory, "We have the *Book of Homilies, The Whole
Duty of Man,* and the *Singing Psalms.*" During the

[2] From *The Five Nations,* by Rudyard Kipling, c. 1903, 1931,
reprinted with permission of Mrs. Kipling and Doubleday, Doran
and Company, Inc.

years following this questionnaire, however, **various** clergymen opened little schools, and it was to these schools, usually taught in the minister's own home, that the founders of the American republic went for their first formal scholastic training. Washington, Randolph, John Marshall, and nearly every other young giant of those days received their first schooling at the hands of a minister. The point is significant and has not been made enough of. For it accounts in part, at least, for the religious idealism which lay at the basis of their future efforts for political freedom.

At five young Thomas Jefferson entered one of these schools where he learned English and the rudiments of mathematics. At nine his father entered him in a Latin school, fourteen miles from Shadwell and conducted by James Maury, a Whig clergyman whom Thomas afterward described as "a correct classical scholar." Under him during the next five years he became well grounded in Greek, Latin, and French, and the English Bible.

College. At seventeen young Jefferson entered William and Mary College, where, says Francis Hirst, "he was speedily beset by all the temptations that assail and still assail young gentlemen of wealth in Virginia and elsewhere." In his autobiography Jefferson gives his own account of his two years in William and Mary.

In the spring of 1760 I went to William and Mary College, where I continued for two years. It was my great good fortune, and what probably fixed the desti-

nies of my life, that Dr. William Small of Scotland
was then Professor of Mathematics, a man profound
in most of the useful branches of science, with a happy
talent of communication, correct and gentlemanly manners, and an enlarged and liberal mind. He, most
happily for me, became soon attached to me, and made
me his daily companion when not engaged in the school;
and from his conversation I got my first views of the
expansion of science, and of the system of things in
which we are placed. Fortunately, the philosophical
chair became vacant soon after my arrival in college,
and he was appointed to fill it *per interim:* and he was
the first who ever gave, in that college, regular lectures
in Ethics, Rhetoric, and Belles-Lettres. He returned to
Europe in 1762, having previously filled up the measure
of his goodness to me, by procuring for me, from his
most intimate friend, George Wythe, a reception as a
student of law, under his direction, and introduced me
to the acquaintance and familiar table of Governor
Fauquier, the ablest man who had ever filled that office.
With him, and at his table, Dr. Small and Mr. Wythe,
his *amici omnium horarum,* and myself, formed a *partie
quarree,* and to the habitual conversations on these occasions I owed much instruction. Mr. Wythe continued
to be my faithful and beloved mentor in youth, and my
most affectionate friend through life.[3]

At the end of the first year there Jefferson realized
with some remorse that he had spent too much time and
money on dress and horses, so he wrote to his guardian
requesting him to charge the entire expense of the year

[3] Francis Hirst: *Life and Letters of Thomas Jefferson,* pp. 25,
26. New York: The Macmillan Company, 1926.

17

not against his father's whole estate, but to Thomas' private share in it. But the guardian generously replied, "If you have sowed your wild oats in this way, the estate can well afford to pay the bill."

His second year he employed more diligently than the first, giving up his gay companions, his riding horse, and even his violin. He devoted fifteen hours a day to his studies, and for exercise ran a mile out of the city and back every evening at twilight. During his vacations at Shadwell, according to Hirst, he devoted three-fourths of each day to his books, "arising at dawn as soon as the hands of the clock on the bedroom mantle-piece could be distinguished in the gray light." By this rigorous discipline he completed the entire college course at the end of the second year.

Yet he was no "grind." He was simply a youth who had begun to find himself and in whom ambition was stirring. He loved languages, and mastered Greek, Latin, and French while still in his teens. To them he later added a fair knowledge of Spanish and Italian. He liked poetry and read much of it, preferring it in the language in which it was originally written. He cared little for fiction, but selected well the novels he read. These included the works of Fielding, Smollett, Sterne, and Cervantes.

Dr. Small. But the most important single element in his years at William and Mary was his personal companionship with Dr. Small and George Wythe. We know little of Small beyond the reference already

18

quoted from Jefferson's autobiography, except that he was also a friend of Erasmus Darwin, grandfather of Charles Darwin. But Jefferson in another passage says that to Small's "enlightened and affectionate guidance of my studies while at college, I am indebted for everything." Referring to the dinners at Governor Fauquier's house—and it was Dr. Small who had introduced him to the Governor—Jefferson wrote: "I have heard (there) more good sense, more rational and philosophical conversation than in all my life besides. They were truly Attic societies. The Governor was musical also, and a good performer; and associated me with two or three other amateurs in his weekly concerts."

George Wythe. George Wythe shared both the scientific interests and the liberal political views of Small and Fauquier. Although without formal schooling himself, he became the greatest lawyer and teacher of law in the colonies. He taught not only Thomas Jefferson, but John Marshall and Henry Clay. He carried his liberal political views into practice and during his own lifetime emancipated the slaves on his own plantation and made provision for their subsistence. Hirst says of him: "So inflexible was his integrity, so warm his patriotism, such his devotion to liberty and to the natural rights of man, that he might be called the Virginian Cato, but for a disinterested liberality which contrasted with the avarice of the Roman."

The next five years Jefferson read law under this

George Wythe at Williamsburg. His letters tell of "mirth and jollity . . . of riding, dancing, and fiddling . . . of disorders in the college followed by expulsions . . . of the opening of the law courts October, 1763, 'which I must attend constantly,' of shorthand, and of various inconsequential love affairs." [4]   But all the while he was becoming indoctrinated with Wythe's teaching about popular rights and religious liberty. He was reading Coke and Locke. He was making friends with Patrick Henry and other young lawyers of the day. He heard young Henry win his first big success in court in a case in which a clergyman had sued for his salary to be paid in tobacco according to contract instead of the currency of the day, which was a fluctuating and insecure medium of exchange. Patrick Henry took the side against the clergyman, and after a stammering and awkward beginning, delivered a speech of such eloquence against the King and his royal clergy that the latter were "driven in a flutter from the crowded courthouse" and Henry was borne off in triumph on the shoulders of the cheering crowd.

Researches in Law. Jefferson was not content with the usual law studies. His inquiring mind sent him back to the original precedents. He studied Anglo-Saxon "in order to trace out for himself the origin of the common law." He formed the habit of writing in a notebook the results of these researches. Describing the process in a reminiscence fifty years later, he

[4] Hirst: *Op. cit.*, p. 30.

says of these records: "They were written at a time of life when I was bold in the pursuit of knowledge, never fearing to follow the truth and reason to whatever results they led, and bearding every authority which stood in their way." His particular research concerning the origin of the common law of England led him to a significant conclusion, and to an answer to the question whether, as was customarily supposed, Christianity was a part of the common law. Jefferson's researches revealed "that the common law was introduced by the Saxons on their settlement in England in the fifth century," whereas they only embraced Christianity between 598 and 686 A.D. Thus he proved that the common law had been in existence in England for two hundred years before Christianity. By such studies he not only developed his mind, but made strong the foundation of his own convictions on the subject of religious freedom and the desirability of separation of church and state.

A Schedule for Study. His own prodigious industry gave him the authority to draw up a course of study which he suggested to Madison and Monroe and other young friends about to enter on their college training.

1. Till eight in the morning employ yourself in Physical studies, namely Agriculture, Chemistry, Anatomy, Zoology, Botany, Ethics, and Natural Religion, Religion Sectarian and Natural Law. . . .

2. From eight to twelve read Law. [Here Jefferson traces a general course of reading in the Common Law

and Chancery and gives a list of law books. He then suggests a case method of study.]

3. From twelve to one read Politics. [Here he proposes a specific list of significant books.]

4. In the afternoon read History. This course comprises the Greek and Latin historians in the original, and a number of English and American writers. . . .

5. From dark to bedtime. The last hours of the day or rather night are assigned to belles-lettres, criticism, rhetoric, and oratory. Among poets "Shakespeare must be singled out by one who wishes to learn the full powers of the English language." [5]

This was the sort of discipline Jefferson had learned under George Wythe. After five years of such study he was admitted to the bar in 1767, and began the practice of law. At that time he was one of the best read men in Virginia. He had mastered legal philosophy as well as facts and cases. The breadth and depth of his knowledge of law rooted here in his training under Wythe came to fruit later in his reform of the Virginia Code, in his diplomatic correspondence in France, and even more in his dispatches as Secretary of State.

Young Lawyer. Look at the young lawyer now. Twenty-four years of age, he stands six feet two inches in height, and is possessed of something of his father's extraordinary muscular strength. His hair is red, his eyes hazel gray, his face kindly, his temper under control, his whole bearing so courtly and dignified that it was said of him that he never gave a personal insult or had occasion to repel one. His children and grandchildren have testified "that they never heard him raise his voice to an angry pitch." He has a profound culture in the sense in which Matthew Arnold used that term connoting a passion for perfection. He reads Homer and the Greek philosophers and playwrights in the original. He is exceptionally proficient in mathematics. He has a talent for mechanical inventions and is deeply interested in music and architecture. Yet he is not without weaknesses. Chief of these is his voice, which becomes husky and inarticulate when raised above the pitch of conversation. He is much too shy by nature to engage sucessfully in parliamentary debate, but he is gifted with an unusual power of written expression and is the master of a clear and forceful style. As Felix Adler says of him, he is to walk through life pen in hand.

Bashful Lover. His shyness involved him in at least one amusing love affair—amusing to us, but tragic to him. Early in his twentieth year he had fallen desperately in love with Rebecca Burwell. He made two attempts to proclaim his passion. Dressed up in all of his finery with a much rehearsed speech in his head, he approached the lady at a dance in the Raleigh Tavern. In her presence he forgot everything he had intended saying and fled from the scene. Several months later he again approached her with a clear and logical presentation of his case, which he wound up by saying that the "decision rested with her and that a new interview would not serve any purpose." [6] Too bashful to force a reply, he left, and indirectly learned a few weeks later of his rejection when the man to whom she gave herself in marriage asked Jefferson to be best man at the wedding. He did not indulge in the comfort of psychopathic, suicidal, or vengeful reactions; the incident only helped to mature him. It made him more than ever throw himself into his work.

His Wife. At twenty-nine he courted and married Martha Skelton, a pretty twenty-three-year-old widow who was to bring him much happiness. She, too, was well read and a lover of the beautiful. She was also an extremely efficient housekeeper whom the large retinue of slaves came to love. Two years before their marriage, Jefferson's home, Shadwell, had burned, and only his favorite violin was saved. He had started the erection of a new home on Monticello (the adjacent "Little Mountain") and now pushed it to completion in time for his marriage.

Monticello. All the power of his disciplined mind and his classical culture he brought to bear upon the construction of this house. Although at the time he built it he was journeying back and forth to the Capitol at Williamsburg to plead his cases before the General Court, his designs and original drawings show a mechanical precision and a feeling for classic harmony

---

[6] Gilbert Chinard: *Thomas Jefferson,* p. 17. Boston: Little, Brown & Co., 1929.

and order.   He had read Palladio's four books of architecture and followed the great Italian in his fundamental conception of "architecture as the imitator of
nature."   It is the essence of classical architecture to
be at home in its surroundings, and Jefferson as architect in his plans for Monticello and later for the State
Capitol and for the University of Virginia had this
sense of appropriateness.   Monticello was and still is
a gem of architectural beauty.   Jefferson planned the
landscaping as well as the house, and together they
formed a home of beauty and dignity not surpassed in
America.   A Frenchman who had enjoyed its generous
hospitality remarked that Mr. Jefferson was "the first
American who had consulted the fine arts to find out
how to shelter himself from the weather." [7]   The house
sheltered not only Jefferson's large household, but the
6,500 books which he had personally collected and which
were not surpassed in quality in any other private
library.

When Jefferson built Monticello he expected that it
would be his home for the rest of his life.   He could
not know that the next forty years were to be devoted
to the public service and away from home.   That
career of public service was punctuated every little
while by retirement to Monticello.   But the retirements
were never of long duration.   The days he spent there
were probably the happiest that he knew.   There his

[7] Francis Hirst: *Life and Letters of Thomas Jefferson*, p. 501.
New York: The Macmillan Company, 1926.

two daughters, Martha and Maria, were born. There four of his children died. There just eleven years after his marriage, his wife died in childbirth. There he lived on, caring not only for his own children but for his widowed sister and her six children.

We may have dwelt too long upon his preparation for the struggle in which he is soon to engage, but how else can we understand the strength and power which he is to display in that struggle? Only for the next seven years does he practice law. His cases in those seven years amounted to almost a thousand, and the average income from them close to three thousand dollars a year—a large income for his day. During this same period he collected and classified many of the early Virginia statutes. But by 1774 the ferment of rebellion was stirring through the colonies, and where could the rebels find a better champion than in this young lawyer whose thirty-one years had trained him to understand and sympathize with their cause and to write and speak with authority?

His Purpose. Those thirty-one years had gradually shaped a great purpose in his mind. During the next forty years of public service that purpose never varied. Stated simply, it was to secure and defend the rights of man. He believed in the dignity and sacredness of man. Man, he felt, could not develop his highest possibilities under any form of tyranny. He must be free. The freedom he needed, however, was far more than political freedom. It included freedom of the mind from ignorance and of the conscience from ecclesiastical bondage. Later Jefferson's purpose became concrete and specific in his efforts to found a public school system topped by a system of public universities. It extended to absolute toleration in religion, even of atheism. It inspired his unsuccessful efforts to free the slaves and his successful one to separate church and state in the young nation. Professor Muzzey is certainly right when he says: "Jefferson's abiding and enthusiastic devotion was to a program of social reform for the accomplishment of which all political measures were but convenient agencies. The appreciation of this fact is fundamental to a systematic study of Jefferson's career." [8] Whether history will eventually vindicate Jefferson's faith in democracy as a means of guaranteeing the rights of man, is not a certainty. There are cynics enough who declare that the American party machine has already confuted him. But if there are cynics now, what word is strong enough to characterize his opposition in the 1790's?

The Opposition. Consider that opposition. Every privileged group in America bitterly opposed Jefferson's monstrous idea that any but the chosen few, the high born, the wealthy, the educated, could be safely entrusted with real liberty to govern themselves or others. The majority of the intellectuals, the lawyers, the doctors, the professors, the preachers, the wealthy—in fact, all the powerful—were against

[8] From an article in the *New York Times*, July 4, 1926, p. 6.

him and his generous principles. The intellectuals and professional men in general opposed them because of the same conceit that makes educated people today think that their higher opportunities must have combined with higher abilities to create their superiority. But the clergy had also a private grievance against him; the Established Church, tax-supported, had meant smooth sailing for those called to preach, "Blessed are ye poor," but Jefferson sought to disestablish the church, and his "atheist law," as they called it, would make sailing all the rougher, because it put them to the necessity of having to think to defend their faith and to make their churches so useful that their people would be willing to support them by voluntary contributions. Nor was it only the Anglican clergy who were to oppose him. In Yankee Connecticut the Congregational clergy were stoutly defending the established order, "laying the lash of their furious denunciation on the backs of the critics." The bankers and the traders of the towns and cities always opposed any proposition that would tend to give the farmers more power. In the days ahead, many of this class will grow rich by gambling on the fluctuations of the new currency. Jefferson will oppose them and they will fight him bitterly. Against this powerful group who control tenaciously the presses of the nation, the only available media of public opinion, Jefferson's potential followers are the farmers and workers of the land, with little class-consciousness, less organization, limited wealth, small influence, and no precedent for action. But they **are** ninety per cent of the population, and Jefferson, with his backwoods sixth sense, understands the potential power of the nation in them. The personification of this privileged class opposition to Jefferson will be one of the most brilliant figures in American history, the keenness of whose intellect ranked him among the giants of finance—Alexander Hamilton. But that colossal contest is twenty years in the future. We shall come to it later.

First Battles. What could young Thomas Jefferson accomplish in the face of such opposition? What part did he play in the struggle for freedom? The full record would take volumes. We have space here for only the barest outline. For we are concerned not so much with his external accomplishments as with the power that resided somewhere within.

At twenty-six years of age—in the year 1769—Jefferson was elected to represent Albermarle County in the Virginia House of Burgesses. The session lasted only five days, for the Burgesses introduced resolutions declaring against taxation without representation and for concerted action with other colonies. Also against deportation from the colonies to Great Britain of persons accused of treason. Thereupon the new royal governor promptly dissolved the House of Burgesses. In that brief time, however, Jefferson suffered two defeats. His draft address to the new governor **had been rejected**, and his bill **to permit slave owners**

29

to free their slaves had been defeated. After the dissolution of the House of Burgesses, eighty-eight of its one hundred ten members met to form an association to boycott certain articles of British trade, so long as the Townshend duties on tea, glass, paper, etc., remained in force. This group of eighty-eight included four young men by the names of George Washington, Richard Henry Lee, Patrick Henry, and Thomas Jefferson.

In the Continental Congress. At the age of thirty-two—in the year 1775—Jefferson was elected one of the Virginia representatives to the Continental Congress. Only two members of the Congress were younger than he. John Adams spoke of him as "prompt, frank, explicit, and decisive upon committees." He seldom, if ever, argued publicly for his or other measures, hating what he called "the morbid rage of debate." But he exercised his pen to good purpose. During this period he wrote a pamphlet entitled "A Summary View of the Rights of America," which attacked the supremacy of Parliament and the errors of the Crown. A few lines from it will illustrate its refreshing difference from the usual method of addressing royalty:

Open your breast, sire, to liberal and expanded thought. Let not the name of George the Third be a blot on the page of history. The whole art of government consists in the art of being honest. Only aim to do your duty, and mankind will give you credit where you fail.[9]

* Hirst: *Op. cit.,* p. 76.

30

Such language was regarded as too radical for acceptance by the majority of delegates. But it got into print and may have been one of the reasons why when war broke out a company of British soldiers was sent to Monticello to capture young Jefferson.

The Declaration of Independence. In the following year during the Second Continental Congress the Virginia representatives moved that the colonies declare themselves independent of Great Britain. After a stirring debate the motion was adopted and a committee appointed to draft the declaration. The committee were John Adams, Benjamin Franklin, Richard Sherman, Robert Livingstone, and Thomas Jefferson—Jefferson receiving more votes than any other. The members of the committee, recognizing the quality of his mind and his forceful power of expression, asked Jefferson to draft the Declaration. Thereupon he secluded himself in his two-room lodgings (for which he paid thirty-five shillings—approximately $8.75 a week), and on a desk of his own design proceeded to write the charter of our liberties. It was a labor of twenty days. The result is one of the immortal documents in the history of human liberty. Although every schoolboy has read it, we must give at least a part of it here, for its picture of the intolerable situation in which the colonists found themselves, and for its reflection of the clear mind of Jefferson.

When, in the course of human events, it becomes necessary for one people to dissolve the political bands

31

which have connected them with another, and to assume among the powers of the earth the separate and equal station to which the laws of nature and of nature's God entitle them, a decent respect to the opinions of mankind requires that they should declare the causes which impel them to the separation.

We hold these truths to be self-evident: that all men are created equal; that they are endowed by their Creator with certain inalienable rights; that among these are life, liberty, and the pursuit of happiness; that to secure these rights, governments are instituted among men, deriving their just powers from the consent of the governed; that whenever any form of government becomes destructive of these ends, it is the right of the people to alter or to abolish it, and to institute new government, laying its foundation on such principles, and organizing its powers in such form, as to them shall seem most likely to effect their safety and happiness. Prudence, indeed, will dictate that governments long established should not be changed for light and transient causes; and accordingly all experience hath shewn that mankind are more disposed to suffer while evils are sufferable, than to right themselves by abolishing the forms to which they are accustomed. But when a long train of abuses and usurpations pursuing invariably the same object, evinces a design to reduce them under absolute despotism, it is their right, it is their duty, to throw off such government, and to provide new guards for their future security. Such has been the patient sufferance of these colonies; and such is now the necessity which constrains them to alter their former systems of government.

The Declaration then enumerates the specific tyrannies of George III, as a result of which he is judged "unfit to be the ruler of a free people," and concludes:

We, therefore, the representatives of the United States of America, in General Congress assembled, appealing to the Supreme Judge of the world for the rectitude of our intentions, do, in the name, and by the authority of the good people of these colonies, solemnly publish and declare, that these united colonies are, and of right ought to be, free and independent states; that they are absolved from all allegiance to the British crown, and that all political connection between them and the state of Great Britain is, and ought to be, totally dissolved; and that as free and independent states, they have full power to levy war, conclude peace, contract alliances, establish commerce, and to do all other acts and things which independent states may of right do.

And for the support of this declaration, with a firm reliance on the protection of Divine Providence, we mutually pledge to each other our lives, our fortunes, and our sacred honour.

Of this document most historians agree with Hirst, who says: "Jefferson's studied prose reveals in its grandeur of purpose and depth of thought a noble response to the national call. Successful at the moment, fortunate in the event, it is and will remain the most cherished possession of republican America." [10]

In the same year Jefferson drafted a new constitution for Virginia, calling it "The New Model." In it he began by deposing George III in language similar to that of the Declaration of Independence, and went on

[10] Hirst: *Op. cit.*, p. 123.

33

to free his state from the vestiges of feudalism in the laws of entail, from the English custom of bequeathing large tracts of land from generation to generation by the law of primogeniture, from supporting an established church by taxation, and from many other special privileges inherited from earlier times.

The following year Jefferson decided to concentrate his efforts in Virginia instead of in the congress, and accepted a seat in the Virginia legislature. There he fathered a bill to reorganize the courts of justice, and saw it passed. With the aid of George Wythe and Edmund Pendleton he revised the whole body of Virginia law. He introduced three bills to provide an elementary and secondary educational system and to enlarge the College of William and Mary into a university, and to provide for the establishment of a public library. For the conviction within him that a democracy must rest upon an educated citizenry had deepened. He introduced another bill consolidating and liberalizing slavery laws, but saw it defeated.

Virginia Statute of Religious Freedom. But his most important work in the Virginia legislature was his bill to establish religious freedom. In it he embodied his ideal of perfect toleration. He held that legislators and rulers are not justified in assuming domination over the faith of others. Genuine religion did not need the support of government. "Truth can stand by itself." After a preamble of clear reasoning and close logic developing this premise, the bill reads:

34

We, the General Assembly of Virginia, do enact, That no man shall be compelled to frequent or support any religious worship, place, or ministry whatsoever, nor shall be enforced, restrained, molested, or burthened in his body or goods, nor shall otherwise suffer, on account of his religious opinions or belief; but that all men shall be free to profess, and by argument to maintain, their opinions in matters of religion, and that the same shall in no wise diminish, enlarge, or affect their civil capacities." [11]

All this may sound trite and commonplace to us today, but it was "the first law ever passed by a popular assembly giving perfect freedom of conscience."

Governor of Virginia. At the age of thirty-six in the year 1779—the dark hour of the South in the war—Jefferson became governor of Virginia, succeeding Patrick Henry. He was re-elected in 1780-81. It was a stormy period. British armies were in possession of Virginia ports and were raiding Virginia plantations. The treasury was empty and the currency was depreciating. Washington called upon the state not only to protect itself but to contribute a large quota of soldiers to his armies in the North and South. Jefferson's correspondence with Washington shows the mutual admiration of the two men and the tireless energy with which Jefferson raised troops for Washington, and at the same time somehow managed to provide for state defense and keep the treasury from absolute bankruptcy.

[11] Hirst: *Op., cit.,* p. 140.

"Notes on Virginia." Shortly after the expiration of his second term as governor of Virginia, he had a bad fall from a horse and was laid up for several weeks. During this period of physical incapacity, he began his first and last book, *Notes on Virginia.* The book reflects Jefferson's wide variety of interests and his scientific mind. He begins with a map and description of the physical features of the region, the Mississippi, Missouri, and Ohio Rivers and their commercial value, the mountains, caverns, and waterfalls, and other beautiful scenery. He discusses the economic geology —the quarries, mines, and hot springs. He catalogs the trees and plants of Virginia with special attention to fruits and vegetables. He presents an elaborate study of the quadrupeds and birds. He records his observations concerning the Indians and his reasons for his theory that they probably came from Eastern Asia before that continent was separated from North America. His chapters on anthropology refute the French theory of the degeneracy of Europeans transplanted in America. He argues the case against slavery and maintains that the low morality of the Negroes was not due to natural depravity, but to their lack of education and their economic handicap. He points out, too, the evil effect of slavery upon the white owners. Finally, he sets forth the constitutional history of Virginia and the steps, especially the educational ones, he thinks necessary for the future development of the state.

In Congress Again. When at the age of thirty-eight he was writing this book, he fully expected to remain at Monticello the rest of his life. But within the year his wife died. His grief was overwhelming, at times rendering him insensible. He turned again to public life and in the following year was elected to Congress. As chairman of the Currency Committee he selected the Spanish dollar as the standard coin for the Union, and determined its subdivisions into half dollars, quarters, dimes, nickels, and pennies.

At forty-one Jefferson was sent by Congress to France to assist Benjamin Franklin and John Adams. Together they drafted commercial treaties for their new nation with the nations of the Old World.

Ambassador to France. At forty-two he was appointed to succeed Benjamin Franklin as ambassador to France. He went among the peasants of France to see how they lived. In a letter to his friend Lafayette, he urged the young republican to make a journey from Nismes to Nice. To do it effectually, he wrote, "you must be absolutely incognito; you must ferret the people out of their hovels as I have done, look into their kettles, eat their bread, loll on their beds on pretense of resting yourself, but in fact to find if they are soft. You will feel a sublime pleasure in the course of this investigation and a sublimer one hereafter, when you shall be able to apply your knowledge to the softening of their beds or the throwing a morsel of meat into their kettle of vegetables." When Lafayette and other

37

leaders in the French Revolution sought his counsel, he gave it in terms of moderation, but of courage based upon America's experience. During this period he refinanced American debts in Holland, designed the Capitol at Richmond, and searched out new plants and methods of cultivation for American agriculture. Later the French government decorated him for inventing an improved plow.

Secretary of State. Returning to America at forty-seven, he again hoped to retire to Monticello, but President Washington persuaded him to serve as Secretary of State. In that capacity, which included the duties of Postmaster General, he accelerated the mail service from fifty to a hundred miles a day, and established the United States Mint, locating it at Philadelphia.

But his great business of these years was something vastly more important. It concerned the very nature and trend of American democracy. For the conflict which had been growing during the past twenty years now came to a head. It was the opposition of the commercial and privileged classes against the small business men and farmers of the new nation. Fundamentally it was opposition to Jefferson's convictions concerning democracy. Alexander Hamilton was the spearhead of that opposition. The contest between these two men is probably the most important one in American history —and it continues to this hour.

The Contest with Alexander Hamilton. Alexander

38

Hamilton was born to a French woman in the West Indies of an irregular union, without benefit of clergy, with a man who may have been a certain shiftless Scotchman whose name was Hamilton, or may not. It is one of the ironies of history that this man born so inauspiciously should be the one to oppose Thomas Jefferson, descendant of the proud Randolphs, in one of the most significant struggles in American history, Jefferson championing the cause of the common people and Hamilton the cause of the aristocracy.

Hamilton was undoubtedly a genius. Jefferson was many-sided, erudite, sagacious, and equipped with an unusual development of abilities that we feel in ourselves. Hamilton was "vivacious, eloquent, pushful, Napoleonic in aims and methods, with French morals and English politics." No one has ever had cause to think that Hamilton was not scrupulously honest in his public charges. He was less moral in his private life: he went so far as to publish a pamphlet on his amours with a certain married woman to explain why he had paid large sums of money to her husband.

Hamilton and Jefferson faced each other across the cabinet table of President Washington. Not unfriendly at first, their principles were so diametrically opposed that it was inevitable they should clash. Hamilton, zealous for the interests of the commercial class, was pro-English even so soon after the war. Jefferson was decidedly friendly to the French for their invaluable assistance in the Revolution. The first clash between them came over the relations with these respective countries. Jefferson wanted free trade; Hamilton wanted tariffs for certain American industries, but not for agriculture. From that time on relations in Washington's cabinet became more and more strained. Jefferson became the head of one party; Hamilton of the other. In a letter to Mrs. John Adams, Jefferson stated fairly and dispassionately the differences between the two parties: "Both of our political parties," he wrote, "at least the honest part of them, agree conscientiously in the same object, the public good; but they differ essentially in what they deem the means of promoting that good. One side (the Federalists) fears most the ignorance of the people. The other side (the republican) fears most the selfishness of rulers independent of them." This was the basic difference. Both agreed that the government drew its power from the people, but Hamilton did not trust the people; Jefferson did. Hamilton and his followers were convinced that only men of the upper class were actually fit to govern. Jefferson recognized the dangers from the ignorance of the people, but held that ignorance could be overcome by popular education—hence his labors for a public school system—and by the actual experience of the people in self-government. He thought that overcoming popular ignorance was a lesser task than curbing the greed for power in a privileged class. Hamilton wanted a strong central government, a large army, senators elected for life, and state governors appointed by the President. He was quite willing for the central government to go deeply into debt. He believed in restraint of individual liberty to the extent of restricting freedom of speech and press. Jefferson wanted the government more decentralized in states and counties, always as near as possible to the individual voter. He wanted no restraints on speech and press. He opposed all militarism. He tried to wipe out the public debt. He preached and practiced the strictest economy in government. He conducted the office of Secretary of State with the aid of only four clerks and a messenger. He said: "I place economy among the first and most important of republican virtues, and public debt as the greatest danger to be feared." Hamilton's policies worked for the advancement of the city dwellers; Jefferson's for the great masses who lived in the rural communities. Here were the national beginnings of the rural-urban conflict.

Such differences could not be reconciled. They rooted too deep in the nature of one's faith or lack of faith in the possibilities of the common man. The conflict which had been smoldering for twenty years burst into flames in a series of Federalist papers, in pamphlets pro and con, in political debates, and in newspaper attacks and counterattacks. We cannot detail the struggle here. Claude Bowers has told it vividly in his *Jefferson and Hamilton*. Hamilton at first won. Backed by the industrialists, tariff-supported, and by speculators who had fattened on speculation in the currency, and by the landed aristocracy, he carried the day for his policies and saw them adopted by the government. Jefferson resigned, and at the end of 1793 once more retired to Monticello.

Vice-President. But Hamilton's victory was short-lived. The farmers and small business men who made up the vast bulk of the population soon found that the Federalist policies worked to their disadvantage and impoverishment. After three years they called Jefferson from his retirement and elected him Vice-President (1796-1801), and then, after the bitterest of battles, President for eight years (1801-09). From then on democracy had the upper hand and Hamilton's followers gradually slipped away from him until his brilliant career ended in the famous duel with Aaron Burr.

President. Jefferson was fifty-eight years old when he became President. Seldom, if ever, has any president accomplished more. He stabilized the national finances, reduced the public debt, negotiated the purchase of Louisiana (1803) from Napoleon at the cost of only eleven and a quarter millions of dollars; and he directed the Lewis and Clark expedition to the West— the expedition which more than any other opened the way for the expansion of the United States through the whole territory from the Mississippi Valley to the Pacific Coast.

Then at the age of sixty-six, after forty years of almost continual service in the public cause, Jefferson again retired to his beloved Monticello, saying: "I have the consolation of having added nothing to my private fortune during my public service, and am retiring with hands as clean as they are empty." So empty, indeed, and his private fortune so depleted that he is soon to be practically bankrupt and his last years lived under a darkening shadow of debt. But his work is not yet done. For the next ten years he continues to direct the fight for the democratic cause and for social reform. Even more important, he founds the University of Virginia, drawing the plans for its beautiful neo-classic buildings himself and supervising the construction of its curriculum, and the choice of its faculty. It was the first university in the country to have an elective curriculum, a complete absence of religious tests, and to introduce the honor system in student relations. Modern university technique was in many important respects foreshadowed by this contribution of Jefferson to higher education.

On the fourth of July, 1826, the fiftieth anniversary of the Declaration of Independence, Jefferson died. On the same day John Adams lingered on his own deathbed. Not knowing that earlier his friend and colleague had passed away, his last words were, "Thomas Jefferson still lives." In a very significant sense John Adams spoke truth. Thomas Jefferson still lives, not only as a revered memory, but as a potent influence in our distinctively American view of government and its relations to human rights and needs. Because he charted the course for the America of the future, he will continue to live as long as America shall remain essentially American. For Jefferson's work is not yet finished. It will not be finished so long as the wealth and privileges of this great land are controlled by a few, while the many are deprived of security and often even of a chance to work.

His Philosophy of Life. Looking back over this career we may note certain fundamental principles by which he was guided. Together they make up his philosophy of life—his religion. As we have noted, he centered his life around the purpose to secure and defend the rights of men to be free, to choose their own government, levy their own taxes, build their own temples, determine their own conduct. "I have sworn," he said, "upon the altar of God, eternal hostility against every form of tyranny over the mind of man." His enemies, including most of the clergy of the day, called him an atheist because among the tyrannies he opposed was the tyranny of ecclesiastical bondage. But he did not think of himself as an atheist. He was so profoundly interested in the teachings of Jesus that he collected them in Greek, in Latin, and in the authorized English version, pasting the three side by side in a scrapbook and classifying them under their respective heads. This scrapbook is now published under the title, *Jefferson's Bible*,[12] although he entitled it, *The Life and Morals of Jesus of Nazareth Extracted Text-*

---

[12] *Jefferson's Bible*, edited by Henry Jackson. New York: Boni & Liveright, 1923.

44

ually from the Gospels in the Greek, Latin, and English.
He habitually read it at bedtime. When he had finished
this compilation he wrote: "I am a Christian in the
only sense in which he (Jesus) wishes anyone to be
—sincerely attached to his doctrines in preference to
all others, ascribing to himself every human excellence
and believing he never claimed any other." During
his presidency he prepared for his friend, Dr. Priestly,
a "syllabus of an estimate of the merit of the doctrines
of Jesus compared with those of others." His passion
for freedom thus had at least some of its roots in his
religious thought. Speaking of slavery he once said:
"Indeed I tremble for my country when I reflect that
God is just: that His justice cannot sleep forever."
The opening paragraphs of the Declaration of Independence assert his conviction that the laws of Nature
and Nature's God entitle every people to separate and
equal station. As Professor Muzzey says, he worshiped
and served liberty in every field of human interest,
social, intellectual, religious, educational, and political. A
good life, he held, was the end and aim of philosophy and
of religion. He wished the churches would give more
attention to that and less to what he called the vagaries
of "trinitarian arithmetic." He would like to have seen
the churches purged "of the outward forms of religious
worship, of all the farcial pomp and nonsense with
which they are loaded." To a young namesake he once
wrote six precepts which might have astonished the
New England parsons who had so thundered against

45

his atheism. They ran: "(1) Adore God. (2) Reverence and cherish your parents. (3) Love your neighbor as yourself. (4) Be just. (5) Be true. (6) Murmur not at the ways of Providence."

Lover of Humankind. He was a humane man, a lover of humankind. A charming picture is preserved for us by one of his great-grandchildren: "He would gather fruit for us, seek out the ripest of figs, or bring down the cherries from on high above our heads with a long stick, at the end of which there was a hook and a little net bag." He combined offices of handicapper, timekeeper, and prize giver for races on the lawn and terrace. His ingenuity in devising presents for the children seemed endless. On winter evenings at dusk, before the candles were brought in, he would teach the children games and learn from them some of theirs. "When the candles were brought, all was quiet immediately for he took up his book to read; and we would not speak out of a whisper lest we should disturb him; and generally we followed his example and took a book; and I have seen him raise his eyes from his own book and look around on the little circle of readers and smile." [13] His attitudes as well as his moods were thoroughly democratic. Every schoolboy has read of his dispensing with all the ceremony which attended the office of President, and of his proceeding on horseback, unattended by pomp, to his first in-

[13] Francis Hirst: *Life and Letters of Thomas Jefferson*, p. 513, New York: The Macmillan Company, 1926.

augural. On one occasion he received the Danish ambassador in felt bedroom slippers. When the shocked
ambassador began to defend formality, Jefferson told
the story of the King of Naples who complained to his
minister that court ceremonial was too irksome, and
asked whether he could not be relieved of such misery.
The minister replied: "Your Majesty must remember
that you, yourself, are but a ceremony." Jefferson
was unceremonious because he felt that he was much
more than just a ceremony.

Failures. Have we pictured a man all success without
failure? He would not tolerate such a portrait, for he
bitterly regretted that he never succeeded in establishing
the common school system he dreamed of. He never
saw international trade free from tariff restrictions.
He never was able to bring about the emancipation of
the slaves. Had he succeeded in getting passed the bill
he drafted in 1784, which provided that "after the year
1800 there shall be neither slavery nor involuntary
servitude in any of the said states," the Civil War
might have been eliminated. That bill was defeated by
a single vote. As Jefferson, himself, wrote soon afterward: "The voice of a single individual would have
prevented this abominable crime from spreading itself
over the new country. Thus we see the fate of millions
unborn hanging on the tongue of one man, and heaven
was silent in that awful moment." As an administra-
tor he frequently found himself thwarted in action
because he saw too many sides of every question. He

hated disputes and altercations, and was supersensitive to criticism.

Sources of Power. What were the sources of Jefferson's power? We have already so dealt with them that we need here only to recapitulate. From his mother he inherited the pride and sensitive taste of an aristocrat. From his father he inherited physical strength, energy of mind, capacity for making friendships and improving opportunities. In his early home, too, he was given an admirable scholastic training in his father's library. "I thank on my bended knees," he once said, "him who directed my early education and gave me that rich treasure." His intimate contact with the virgin forest to the West and with the Indians there, and his equally intimate contact with the cultured society on the plantations of Virginia, contributed something toward his breadth of sympathy. The friends and teachers of his youth—James Maury, Peyton Randolph, William Small, and George Wythe—shaped his young mind and lifted his horizons. While he was yet in his teens he learned to budget his time and make every hour of the day count. Travel in various countries gave him insight into the experience of older civilizations and increasing belief in the opportunities for developing a new civilization in America. His enjoyment of the arts, especially of architecture, was probably at the basis of his ability to build Monticello and to design the Capitol at Richmond and the University of Virginia. But those dreams would never

48

have become realities had he not in the meantime developed his practical ability to express his vision and aesthetic taste in terms of drawings and design.

All these are sufficient to account for a man of culture and ability, but not sufficient to account for Thomas Jefferson. The power of Jefferson in his public career lay in his unshakable, almost fanatic, faith in the common man and his single purpose to secure and defend his rights. Some have said that this faith amounted to a religion with him. Rather it was a part of his religion. Religion for him was not mysticism. It was something that goaded him to serve his fellow men and provided a refuge to which he could retreat in times of stress and re-align his action and conform his will "to the laws of Nature and of Nature's God." It gave him that integrity of character that made all men trust his honesty no matter how much they differed from his opinions.

His ability to find rest in his many hobbies, most of which led him into the realm of beauty, provided another source of power. They gave him respite from toil and comfort in defeat. His vast knowledge of men, from the Indians of the frontier to the statesmen of Europe, from the slaves of Virginia to the courts of France, gave him a peculiar sense of mastery of political action. When a bill was passed in Congress he knew what the reaction to it in the backwoods would be weeks before the slow mails could bring a newspaper. At the head of a political party he was a leader rather than a driver. Gently and almost imperceptibly he led many of his opponents to his own views.

Beyond all this and permeating it—his kindness. Felix Adler relates that while President of the United States Jefferson was one day horseback riding with a group of younger friends. The party came to a swollen stream. On the bank sat a poor man looking ruefully at the raging flood he was unable to cross. The man watched the others ford the stream on their horses, but said nothing to them. Last came Jefferson. The man, not recognizing him as President, asked if he might mount behind him and cross the stream. Jefferson cheerfully took him across. On the opposite side someone asked the man why he had not requested the service of one of the other members of the party. He replied: "There are some faces on which is clearly written the answer 'No' to a question you intend to ask. There are other faces on which is written 'Yes.' On their faces was written 'No.' On his 'Yes.'" Therein lay probably his greatest source of power—that answer "Yes" to the insistent, if humble, claim of the common man for his rights.

CHARLES DICKENS

1812-1870

CHARLES DICKENS has at least three claims for admission to any select company of men of power. First, he was a novelist whose works are forever enshrined in the affections of the English-speaking world. Second, he was a social reformer who without sacrificing his art deliberately used it to stir up the emotions of his fellow men and to get them to do something in behalf of child laborers, of men rotting in debtors' prisons, of the poor who were living in unspeakably filthy houses, and of children whose education was being left to cruel and incompetent persons. Third, he was a man who somehow lifted himself above the limitations of bad health in childhood, of uncomprehending parents, of the restrictions of long hours of child labor, and of a late and meager education.

His novels are probably in more homes than those of any other writer. If we could raise the curtain upon a typical scene in tens of thousands of English and

American homes we would see around the fireside a father and mother, probably in their early forties, seated in comfortable chairs; two or three children from six to eighteen stretched out on the hearth rug; and grandpa or grandma reclining on a couch, while mother reads aloud *David Copperfield* or *The Tale of Two Cities* or *Nicholas Nickleby* or *Great Expectations.* Half of them have heard the story before, but hearing it again is to call old joys back to life. Father insists on telling how his boyhood home looked when he first read the story; and grandpa remembers his father telling of the excitement the book caused when it first came out as a serial in a magazine which Dickens edited.

Channing Pollock relates one incident illustrative of that excitement. It concerns *Old Curiosity Shop.* The magazine publishing it came to America by sailing vessel. As the interest in the story mounted from week to week the crowds became larger on the New York wharf waiting to buy copies as soon as the ship docked. By the time the story reached its last chapter these crowds had grown to such numbers and to such a pitch of suspense that they swarmed five or six thousand strong upon the wharf and could not wait until the ship docked. When they spied the captain on the deck they called out across the narrowing water the question that burned in everyone's heart: "Did little Nell die?" A novelist who could produce such an effect had power.

Dickens could never have produced that effect had he

not known intimately the persons and the conditions about which he wrote. His novels, notwithstanding their humor and occasionally uproarious laughter, are productions of pain—his own pain as well as the suffering of myriads of others in his day. Micawber, "waiting for something to turn up" and landing in a debtors' prison, was his own father. Little Nell was his wife's youngest sister. He had known little Dorrit when he was a boy, and David Copperfield was himself. As W. W. Crotch puts it:

It was not, in the case of Dickens, merely that he learnt in suffering what he afterwards taught in prose. The influence was deeper than that. In his narratives he does not describe poverty and pain as a thing apart: he lays bare himself. It is his own broken child-heart which one sees—the picture of his own childish tragedy.[1]

His Father. He was born at Landport in Portsea, England, February 7, 1812. His father, John Dickens, was a genial, energetic, but ineffective soul with a small job in the British navy, a clerkship in the paymaster's office. He was frequently transferred from place to place, but in each instance seems to have managed to accumulate a considerable collection of debts before he was moved on to the next place. He also accumulated children, Charles being the second of eight. Two of the others died in infancy.

[1] W. W. Crotch: *Charles Dickens: Social Reformer,* p. 15. London: Chapman and Hall, Ltd., 1913.

His Mother. Of his mother we know next to nothing. She seems to have been almost a blank so far as personality is concerned. Her son's frequent allusions to Scripture might indicate that his mother was religiously inclined, but what with continual childbearing and endeavoring to look after the household cares of the poverty-stricken family, and moving the household goods every year or so, it is no wonder that she made little impression other than that of an overburdened wifely drudge.

A Sickly Child. Charles was a sickly child. Violent attacks of spasms often kept him in bed for days at a time and disqualified him for outdoor games and association with boys of his own age in play. He watched them from his window, and when he could not see them he read books. He declared in later life that his childish illness had brought him great advantages in that he was thus early turned to books. He had but a year or two in school, but he learned to read and he read everything he could get his hands on, and remembered especially *Tom Jones, The Vicar of Wakefield, Don Quixote, Robinson Crusoe, Arabian Nights,* and *Tales of the Genii.* Such books fed his mind and kindled his imagination. He formed the habit of impersonating the characters and dramatizing their exploits for the entertainment of his younger brothers and sisters. He told stories and sang comic songs so well that he came into demand at children's parties and other gatherings. He also began to write before he was

54

ten years of age, his first attempt being a tragedy, *Misnar, the Sultan of India.*

Even so, his parents did not see sufficient promise in him to continue him in school. His older sister, Fannie, seems to have been the darling of the family, and for her they managed to provide music lessons. But for Charles they felt that further schooling would be a loss of time and money.

His home at this time was at Chatham. Not far from it on the road to Rochester stood a large mansion known as "Gad's Hill Place" at which he used to gaze in wonder. It seemed to him the visible embodiment of the grand castles he had read about in his books. His father, seeing him so fond of it, used to say, "If you were to be very persevering and were to work hard, you might some day come to live in it." But that seemed quite impossible to the queer, sickly little boy who was Charles Dickens. Nevertheless, that very mansion was one day to become his own, but not until he had become even poorer and then toiled the long, hard way out of poverty.

To London Slums. When he was nine the family removed to London, taking a modest house in a shabby part of the city. The contrast between this home and his former one in the country weighed upon his sensitive spirit. He missed the garden, the flowers, the spacious out-of-doors. Everywhere around him were poverty and filth. His easygoing father did as well as he could, but he was unconscious of the needs of the boy who longed for school and for the companionship of books and boys and nature. To his biographer, Forster, Dickens spoke of his misery in these years. He felt himself neglected. He looked to his father for some sort of guidance and help, but his father was always "waiting for something to turn up." He wrote:

I know my father to be as kind-hearted and generous a man as ever lived in the world. Everything that I can remember of his conduct to his wife, or children, or friends, in sickness or affliction is beyond all praise. By me, as a sick child, he has watched night and day, unweariedly and patiently, many nights and days. He never undertook any business, charge, or trust, that he did not zealously, conscientiously, punctually, honorably discharge. His industry has always been untiring. He was proud of me in his way, and had a great admiration of the comic singing. But, in the ease of his temper, and the straitness of his means, he appeared to have utterly lost at this time the idea of educating me at all, and to have utterly put from him the notion that I had any claim upon him, in that regard, whatever. So I degenerated into cleaning his boots of a morning, and my own; and making myself useful in the work of the little house; and looking after my younger brothers and sisters (we were now six in all), and going on such poor errands as arose out of our poor way of living.[2]

His father's affairs going from bad to worse, his mother now made the one supreme effort of her life to

[2] John Forster: *The Life of Charles Dickens*, pp. 11, 12. Philadelphia: J. B. Lippincott Company, 1903. Used by permission.

lift herself out of tragedy and her family out of penury. In their desperate circumstances she announced to the community that she was setting up a school and invited parents of the neighborhood to send their children. Not a child came. Dickens vividly portrays this incident in *David Copperfield*.

At last his father was arrested for debt and sent to prison. Charles was horrified. His boyish soul descended into a hell of humiliation and misery. It fell to his lot to take the household goods one by one to the pawnbrokers and to bargain for loans upon them. This he did until only the beds and a few cheap chairs were left. The pawnbrokers in his novels are not figments of his imagination. They are creatures of flesh and blood who had forever stamped their characters upon his quivering spirit when his body was so small that his scared white face scarcely reached as high as the counter.

A Child Laborer. He was now ten. Practically all the furniture was gone and there was nothing to eat. The rest of the family went to live with the father in the debtors' prison. A cousin offered Charles a job in his shoe-blacking factory, where he could earn six shillings a week by working long hours each day pasting labels on bottles. Dickens says of this experience:

It is wonderful to me how I could have been so easily cast away at such an age. It is wonderful to me that, even after my descent into the poor little drudge I had been since we came to London, no one had compassion enough on me—a child of singular abilities, quick, eager, delicate, and soon hurt, bodily or mentally—to suggest that something might have been spared, as certainly it might have been, to place me at any common school. Our friends, I take it, were tired out. No one made any sign. My father and mother were quite satisfied. They could hardly have been more so if I had been twenty years of age, distinguished at a gram mar school, and going to Cambridge.[3]

No words can express the secret agony of my soul as I sunk into this companionship; compared these everyday associates with those of my happier childhood; and felt my early hopes of growing up to be a learned and distinguished man crushed in my breast. The deep remembrance of the sense I had of being utterly neglected and hopeless—of the shame I felt in my position —of the misery it was to my young heart to believe that, day by day, what I had learned and thought and delighted in, and raised my fancy and my emulation up by, was passing away from me, never to be brought back any more—cannot be written.[4]

Having no home to go to, he found for himself cheap lodgings near the factory. Only by the utmost economy could he manage to eke out a living by his pitiful wages. He says:

I know that I worked, from morning to night, with common men and boys, a *shabby child*. I know that I tried, but ineffectually, not to anticipate my money, and to make it last the week through; by putting it away in a drawer I had in the counting-house, wrapped into six little parcels, each parcel containing the same amount

---

[3] Forster: *Op. cit.*, pp. 17, 18.   [4] *Ibid.*, pp. 18, 19.

and labeled with a different day. I know that I have lounged about the streets insufficiently clad and unsatisfactorily fed. I know that but for the mercy of God, I might easily have been, for any care that was taken of me, a little robber or a little vagabond.[5]

Just how long he lived in this condition we do not know—a matter of months or possibly a year, but it seemed an eternity. Eventually his father received a small legacy, paid his debts, and was released from prison. At almost the same time Charles' sister Fannie won a prize at the Royal Academy of Music. The family fortunes began to look up for everyone but Charles. He tells us that at night when he went to bed the tears ran down his face and he prayed earnestly to be lifted out of his humiliation and neglect. The prayer seems to have been answered. At least his father had a quarrel with the cousin who employed the boy and as a result Charles was discharged.

He accepted the discharge as a boon from heaven, but he reckoned without his mother. In mistaken zeal for peace she called upon the cousin, patched up the quarrel, and came home with a request for Charles to return to work next morning. This only transferred the quarrel to her own home, for her husband declared that Charles should go back no more. He won. If the mother ever again attempted to assert her personality, there is no record of it. Charles could never forget that she so little understood his distress in the degrading surroundings of his work that she was warm for his being sent back. Nor in after years when he had occasion to be in the vicinity of the warehouse could he endure to go near it. The memories were too painful.

To School. His father, now possessed of modest means, yielded to his son's importunities and arranged to send him to school. So at the age of twelve we find Charles in the Wellington House Academy where he remained two years. He has described the school:

A profound impression was made upon me, I remember, by the roar of voices in the schoolroom suddenly becoming hushed as death when Mr. Creakle entered after breakfast, and stood in the doorway looking round upon us like a giant in a storybook surveying his captives. . . .

"Now, boys, this is a new half. Take care what you're about, in this new half. Come fresh up to the lessons, I advise you, for I come fresh up to the punishment. I won't flinch. It will be of no use your rubbing yourselves; you won't rub the marks out that I shall give you. Now get to work, every boy!"

When this dreadful exordium was over . . . Mr. Creakle came to where I sat, and told me that if I were famous for biting, he was famous for biting too. He then showed me the cane, and asked me what I thought of *that,* for a tooth? Was it a sharp tooth, hey? Was it a double tooth, hey? Had it a deep prong, hey? Did it bite, hey? Did it bite? At every question he gave me a fleshy cut with it that made me writhe. . . .

Not that I mean to say these were special marks of distinction, which only I received. On the contrary, a large majority of the boys (especially the smaller ones) were visited with similar instances of notice, as Mr. Creakle made the round of the schoolroom. Half the establishment was writhing and crying, before the day's work began; and how much of it writhed and cried before the day's work was over I am really afraid to recollect, lest I should seem to exaggerate.[6]

In *Household Words* he gives another picture of such a school and tells of the parrots, canaries, linnets, and especially the white mice kept by the boys. The boys trained the mice much better than the master trained the boys. Dickens recalls in particular one white mouse who "lived in the cover of a Latin dictionary, ran up ladders, drew Roman chariots, shouldered muskets, turned wheels, and even made a very creditable appearance on the stage as the Dog of Montargis, who might have achieved greater things but for having had the misfortune to mistake his way in a triumphal procession to the Capitol, when he fell into a deep inkstand, and was dyed black and drowned."

In spite of the cruelty and incapacity of the master of this school, Charles found it an infinitely happier place for him than the shoe-blacking warehouse. His health began to thrive and his spirits to lift. Owen P. Thomas, who was enrolled in the same school, recollected young Dickens as a small but well-built lad "with a more than usual flow of spirits inducing to harmless fun; seldom or never to mischief." He says that Dickens held his head more erect than lads ordinarily

[6] Charles Dickens: *David Copperfield.*

do and that there was a general smartness about him. He had learned to write a good hand with a flourishing signature and his sense of humor had begun to blossom like flowers after a long winter.

At Fifteen a Lawyer's Office Boy. At fifteen we find Charles in the employ of Edward Blackmore, a solicitor. Here he remained for a year and a half picking up a smattering of law, but storing in his memory vivid images of the people who came in and out of lawyers' offices. These people were all to reappear, retouched with Dickens' humor, in his *Pickwick Papers, Nicholas Nickleby, Great Expectations,* and other novels.

He Resolves to Become a Reporter. On leaving the law office Charles determined to become a reporter. He studied shorthand and undertook to supplement his meager education by taking advantage of the facilities of the reading room of the British Museum. Of his difficulties in mastering shorthand he tells us in *David Copperfield.* A friend had told him that to master this skill was no less a task than mastering six languages. But he went at it with a will and persevered.

The changes that were rung upon dots, which in such a position meant such a thing, and in such another position something else entirely different; the wonderful vagaries that were played by circles; the unaccountable consequences that resulted from marks like flies' legs; the tremendous effects of a curve in a wrong place; not only troubled my waking hours, but reappeared before me in my sleep.[7]

[7] Forster: *Op. cit.,* p. 37.

By the time he was nineteen years old he had so mastered shorthand and so developed his skill in description that he obtained a job as reporter for a London newspaper called *The True Sun.* But his connection with this paper seems to be chiefly memorable for the fact that he successfully engineered a reporters' strike. Next he went with the *Mirror of Parliament,* where it was his task to sit in the gallery of Parliament and faithfully transcribe the doings of that deliberative body. He was said to be the best shorthand writer who entered the press gallery. His growing reputation secured him an engagement with a greater paper, *The Morning Chronicle.*

These years as a reporter gave him severe training. They taught him the necessity of accuracy and of concentrated and rapid labor under the most difficult circumstances. They taught him, too, the virtue of concise yet vivid expression. He described them to Forster:

I have pursued the calling of a reporter under circumstances of which my brethren . . . can form no adequate conception. I have often transcribed for the printer from my shorthand notes important speeches in which the strictest accuracy was required and a mistake in which would have been to a young man severely compromising, writing on the palm of my hand by the light of a dark lantern in a post-chaise and four, galloping through a wild country and through the dead of night at the then surprising rate of fifteen miles an hour. . . .

I once "took," as we used to call it, an election speech

of Lord John Russell at the Devon contest in the midst of a lively fight maintained by all the vagabonds in the division . . . and under such a pelting rain that I remember two good-natured colleagues who chanced to be at leisure, held a pocket-handkerchief over my notebook after the manner of a state canopy in an ecclesiastical procession. . . .

Returning home from exciting political meetings . . . to the waiting press in London, I do verily believe I have been upset in almost every description of public vehicle known in this country. . . .

I have charged for broken hats, broken luggage, broken chaises, broken harness—everything but a broken head—which is the only thing they would have grumbled to pay for.[8]

First Published Writing. In December, 1833, when he was twenty-one years old there appeared his first piece of creative writing as distinguished from reportorial writing. It bore the title, *A Dinner at Poplar Walk.* He had placed the manuscript in "a dark letter box up a dark court in Fleet Street, with much fear and trembling. He had addressed it to "the Old Monthly Magazine." To his delight the editor published it. During the next two years he wrote nine sketches for this journal. One of these he signed "Boz." This was the nickname of his favorite brother, Augustus, whom he had dubbed "Moses," which, when pronounced through the nose became "Bozes," and when shortened became "Boz." For these sketches he received nothing

[8] Forster: *Op. cit.,* pp. 40, 41.

64

but the satisfaction of seeing his work in print, the magazine proving a financial failure.

He Wins a Salary Increase. Meanwhile, the *Morning Chronicle* started an evening sheet, in which all the important speeches of Parliament were to be reported verbatim for future reference. Dickens was given a chance to work on this sheet as well as the morning edition, and a promise that his salary would be increased from five to seven guineas a week if he made good on both. He determined to earn that increase. One day Mr. Stanley (afterwards Lord Derby) made a long and important speech on the perennial Irish question. The *Chronicle* assigned eight reporters, including Dickens, to take down the speech. They were to work in relays, each to work forty-five minutes, then to retire and write out his portion and to be succeeded by the next. Fields relates the story:

Young Dickens was detailed to lead off with the first part. It also fell to his lot, when the time came round, to report the closing portions of the speech. On Saturday the whole was given to the press, and Dickens ran down to the country for a Sunday's rest. Sunday morning had scarcely dawned when his father, who was a man of immense energy, made his appearance in his son's sleeping-room. Mr. Stanley was so dissatisfied with what he found in print, except the beginning and ending of his speech (just what Dickens had reported) that he sent immediately to the office and obtained the sheets of those parts of the report. He there found the name of the reporter, which, according to custom, was written on the margin. Then he requested that the young man bearing the name of Dickens should be immediately sent for. . . . In telling the story, Dickens said: "I remember perfectly to this day the aspect of the room I was shown into and the two persons in it, Mr. Stanley and his father. Both gentlemen were extremely courteous to me, but I noted their evident surprise at the appearance of so young a man. While we spoke together, I had taken a seat extended to me in the middle of the room. Mr. Stanley told me he wished to go over the whole speech and have it written out by me, and if I were ready he would begin now. Where would I like to sit? I told him I was very well where I was, and we could begin immediately. He tried to induce me to sit at a desk, but at that time in the House of Commons there was nothing but one's knees to write upon, and I had formed the habit of doing my work in that way. Without further pause he began and went rapidly on, hour after hour, to the end, often becoming very much excited and frequently bringing down his hand with great violence upon the desk near which he stood." [9]

He won the increase in salary!

Two years later he collected his *Sketches by Boz* into two volumes illustrated by Cruikshank and published them. He was able to sell the copyright for a hundred and fifty pounds, an unusually high price for those times when the copyright laws were loose and ineffective. Dickens was nobody's fool when it came to busi-

---

[9] James T. Fields: *Yesterdays with Authors,* pp. 230, 231. Used by permission of, and by arrangement with, Houghton Mifflin Company.

ness. His years of poverty had sharpened his wits where money was concerned.

Finding Himself. He is now fairly launched upon the career that is to make his fame as well as his fortune. Carlyle gives a brief and vivid picture of him:

He is a fine little fellow—Boz, I think. Clear, blue, intelligent eyes, eyebrows that he arches amazingly, large protrusive rather loose mouth, a face of most extreme *mobility,* which he shuttles about—eyebrows, eyes, mouth, and all—in a very singular manner while speaking. Surmount this with a loose coil of common-colored hair, and set it on a small compact figure, very small. . . . For the rest, a quiet, shrewd-looking little fellow, who seems to guess pretty well what he is and what others are.[10]

He has outlived his sickliness of early years. His hardships and trials have developed his will power—the will to live and to make something of himself. Out of the welter of poverty, disaster, and ill-health, and the pitiful example of his father, he has somehow wrought a character, a passion, and a message that are to make him England's favorite writer and foremost champion of the poor, the downtrodden, and the under-privileged. He has known pain, hunger, disappointment, grinding poverty, the misery of unrequited longings and aspirations. In spite of these handicaps he has developed personal traits of order, method, industry, and self-reliance. With a minimum of schooling he

[10] Quoted by W. W. Crotch in his book, *The Secret of Dickens,* p. 121. Chapman and Hall, 1919.

has nevertheless educated himself. We should probably never have heard of him had he gone through the routine educational mill of his day. He will never become a bookish man, but he is a keen observer of men and a passionate student of their ways. As Marzials says, he has acquired "knowledge and sympathy, the seeing eye and the feeling heart"—something that a mere book education could not have given him.

It is too much to expect that he should have been thus educated so abnormally, so greatly at the expense of certain wrenchings and strainings, without having acquired some unlovely traits that render him less winsome and less attractive. Forster speaks of a certain self-assertiveness, an aggressiveness and kind of imperiousness, and a more or less fierce intolerance of advice. These traits mar an otherwise magnetic character. No human is perfect, and it is some comfort to the rest of us to learn that this man who consorted with the gods had some of the defects of the human family.

Marriage. The year 1836, when he was twenty-four, is memorable in Dickens' life for two events: his marriage and the appearance of Mr. Pickwick. He married Catherine Hogarth, daughter of George Hogarth, musical and dramatic critic of the *Morning Chronicle.* There had been a previous, rather shadowy, love affair in Dickens' life which, while it is hardly worth mentioning, yet belongs in the picture if we are to have an honest one. We know little about it except that the girl was the basis of the character Dora, the tragic child-wife in *David Copperfield,* and that to his meeting with this first love years afterward we are indebted for certain passages in *Little Dorrit.*

Sam Weller and Fame. The first sketches of Pickwick, illustrated by Seymour, appeared in the spring of this year. They created no sensation. The publishers were debating whether or not to discontinue the series when suddenly Sam Weller appeared on the scene, and disaster was turned into success. The genial Sam saved the day. All contemporary accounts agree that the success was sudden and enormous. Dickens, not yet twenty-four, awoke to find himself famous. He sprang immediately to the peak of popularity. From four hundred copies of Part I of Pickwick the printing rose to forty thousand copies of Part XV. Everybody wanted it. It was laughed over from one end of the kingdom to the other. It was talked about everywhere. Critics said that a new and vital force in English literature had come to birth.

The time was ripe for a new pen in English literature. Byron was dead, as were also Shelley, Keats, Coleridge, and Lamb. Southey was declining. Wordsworth had done his best work. Carlyle had just published his *Sartor Resartus* and was full of promise of power, but he had not yet published his *French Revolution* nor delivered his lectures on the *Heroes.* Macaulay, Tennyson, and Browning were coming, but their stars were still below the horizon. Sir Walter Scott had been dead five years, and his novels were popular, but their people and plots were of the Middle Ages rather than of contemporary life. Charlotte Brontë, Charles Kingsley, George Eliot were yet to be heard from. There was then a conspicuous vacancy in the line of novelists.

The Man, the Hour, the Book. Why did *Pickwick* make such an immediate hit? Frank Marzials, in his book, *Dickens,* has given probably the most satisfactory answer. Writing while its first impact on the public mind was clear in his memory, he says that "the admirable freshness of the book won its way into every heart. There is a fervor of youth and healthy good spirits about the whole thing." Byron had uttered "his wail of despair over a worthless world," but for Dickens the world was not worthless. Life was pleasant, challenging, something to be enjoyed, not endured. He reveled in it and all the queer quirks of the human beings around him. He affected no superiority toward them or their ways of life. The characters in *Pickwick* were filled with animal spirits and they cavorted over the English landscape like lambs gamboling. Dickens loved his characters. He surrounded them all with his affections. He looked at them as a good father looks at his children, delighted with their attempts to walk, tolerant of their failings, amused at their pranks, sorrowful when they encounter the "slings and arrows of outrageous fortune."

And above all there was Dickens' "royal gift of humor," a gift that could place the most dignified characters in the most ridiculous situations, and with equal fun the most stupid and eccentric characters in dignified situations. By his humor he made even the dullest characters amusing. Yet nowhere in *Pickwick* or in any other of his novels did he make sport of anything worthy of respect. He had a clear distinction in his own mind between right and wrong and never mixed the two. His humor is always wholesome, genial, and kindly. He knew—no one better—that humanity has its cancers and its plague-spots. But he knew also what so few modern writers seem to have learned, that pointing a cynical finger at those plague spots gets us nowhere. Dickens pictures the plague spots of England as no one else has ever done, but never with cynicism. He delighted "in finding some touch of goodness, some lingering memory of better things, some hopeful aspiration, some trace of unselfish devotion in characters where all seems sodden and lost. In brief, the laughter is the laughter of one who sees the foibles and even the vices of his fellow men, and yet looks on them lovingly and helpfully."

Pickwick Papers made twenty thousand pounds for the publishers. They had been inclined to feel that they had been too generous when they had paid him one hundred fifty pounds for his *Sketches by Boz*. Now they were willing to risk a hundred times that.

Full Steam Ahead. During the next four years Dickens took every advantage of his conquest of the literary world and worked at top speed. The quantity

71

of his work in these five years is amazing. He wrote a pamphlet on Sabbatarianism; a farce in two acts—*The Strange Gentleman*—for St. James Theater; a comic opera—*The Village Coquette*—the music, of course, written by another; *Oliver Twist* and *Nicholas Nickleby*. In fact his output was so voluminous that the *Quarterly Review* warned him that he was writing too much and too crudely, and that as he had risen like a rocket he was in danger of coming down like the stick. Dickens accepted the criticism in good spirit. He continued his work strenuously, but improved his quality.

Riches. He waxed rich. He moved to better chambers and here in Gray's Inn his wife presented him with their first-born son on January 6, 1837. Shortly afterward they moved to yet larger quarters, a house in Regent's Park. This home became a rendezvous for the principal literary men and women of London. Washington Irving, Bulwer-Lytton, Wilkie Collins, William Makepeace Thackeray, George Eliot, and a whole host of lesser figures gathered here from time to time, and the neighborhood rang with their laughter.

He developed peculiar habits of work. He preferred the early morning hours for his writing. He had a great penchant for walking. He knew his London and loved to roam and prowl about it at night. The dark streets and alleys fascinated him. He found refreshment and recreation in these night walks about the

72

city streets. The opening passage of *Old Curiosity Shop*
has more than a touch of autobiography in it:

> Night is generally my time for walking. In the sum-
> mer I often leave home early in the morning, and roam
> about fields and lanes all day, or even escape for days
> or weeks together, but saving in the country I seldom
> go out until after dark, though, Heaven be thanked, I
> love its light and feel the cheerfulness it sheds upon the
> earth, as much as any creature living.[11]

He gave himself no rest between novels. As soon as
he finished one he started another—or even before. He
completed *Old Curiosity Shop* on January 17, 1841,
and began *Barnaby Rudge* the following week. These
two novels both appeared in serial form in the fashion
of the continued story of today. Dickens first popu-
larized that form. Whatever happened in his own life
during the writings of a book was apt to find its way
between its covers. Thus about the time he began the
Old Curiosity Shop his sister-in-law, Mary Hogarth,
a girl of seventeen whom he loved dearly, died. He
immortalized her in the person of Little Nell.

To America. After five years of this feverish writing he was seized with wanderlust—a desire to "go
places and see things"—that never afterward entirely
forsook him. Until now he had never had enough
money to travel anywhere. But Fortune was smiling
and America was beckoning. Washington Irving had

[11] Dickens: *Old Curiosity Shop.*

written enthusiastic comments on *Old Curiosity Shop* and had invited Dickens to visit him. The prospect of getting new ideas for a book and of seeing a great new country, as well as being lionized at receptions, appealed to Dickens. He loved being lionized. Applause, after his early years of neglect, to him was as the manna in the wilderness to the Hebrew children. So with his wife, Catherine, he set sail for America in January, 1842, leaving his four children at home in the care of a nurse, housekeeper, and some friends who agreed to act as foster-parents. After a stormy voyage of fourteen days, he landed at Halifax and was received with regal honors. Boston showed even greater enthusiasm. Writing to a friend about it Dickens said: "How can I give you the faintest notion of my reception here; of the crowds that pour in and out the whole day; of the people that line the streets when I go out; of the cheering when I went to the theater; of the copies of verses, letters of congratulation, welcomes of all kinds, balls, dinners, assemblies without end?" [12] Fields, who saw him on his arrival in Boston says that he ran or rather flew up the steps of the hotel and sprang into the hall:

He seemed all on fire with curiosity, and alive as I never saw mortal before. From top to toe every fiber of his body was unrestrained and alert. What vigor, what keenness, what freshness of spirit, possessed him! He laughed all over, and did not care who heard him! He seemed like the Emperor of Cheerfulness on a cruise

[12] Forster: *Op. cit.*, pp. 136, 137.

of leisure, determined to conquer a realm or two of fun every hour of his overflowing existence.[13]

Wherever he went the gayest of young writers and artists gathered about him and "showed him the town." Says Fields: "Dickens kept up one continuous shout of uproarious laughter as he went rapidly forward reading the signs on the shops and observing the architecture of the new country into which he had dropped as if from the clouds." Deputations from the far west (St Louis was "far west" to Dickens) called upon him. Others came, he says, "from the lakes, the rivers, the backwoods, the log houses, the cities, the factories, villages, and towns." He was honored by universities, by Congress, and by other bodies public and private of every sort. He held a regular levee in his hotel wherever he went and shook hands with five or six hundred people on every such occasion. He rode the crest of the wave of popularity and at first found America altogether enchanting. He was delighted at the absence of beggars on the street and at the comfortable homes of the people, even the toilers.

He wanted to see everything. "I go into the prisons, the police offices, the watchhouses, the hospitals, the workhouses. I was out half the night in New York with two of their most famous constables; started at midnight, and went into every brothel, thieves' house,

[13] James T. Fields: *Yesterdays with Authors,* p. 128. Used by permission of, and by arrangement with, Houghton Mifflin Company.

murdering hovel, sailors' dancing-place, and abode of villainy, both black and white, in town." [14]

But as the weeks stretched into months and his hard traveling wore upon his nerves, he began to register discontent with the new country. To his friend W. C. Macready in England he wrote:

It is of no use; I *am* disappointed. This is not the republic I came to see; this is not the republic of my imagination. I infinitely prefer a liberal monarchy— even with its sickening accompaniment of Court circles —to such a government as this. The more I think of its youth and strength, the poorer and more trifling in a thousand aspects it appears in my eyes. In everything of which it has made a boast, excepting its education of the people, and its care for poor children, it sinks immeasurably below the level I had placed it upon, and England, even England, bad and faulty as the old land is, and miserable as millions of her people are, rises in the comparison. . . . Freedom of opinion; where is it? I see a press more mean and paltry and silly and disgraceful than any country I ever knew. . . . In the respects of not being left alone, and of being horribly disgusted by tobacco chewing and tobacco spittle, I have suffered considerably.[15]

The farther he traveled the greater grew his distaste for America. He was irked by what he called "American brag," "American hunger for dollars," and the lack of culture as evidenced by the American indifference

[14] *A Collection of Letters of Dickens,* p. 26. New York: Charles Scribner's Sons, 1889.
[15] *Ibid.,* p. 20.

to art and literature. Yet Americans idolized him and were lavish in the honors and the money they paid to him.

Reverses. When he returned to England he wrote his *American Notes* and *Martin Chuzzlewit,* both highly critical of America. Here he met his first great setback. The *Notes* sold fairly well, but *Chuzzlewit* poorly. People had come to look for lovable characters in Dickens' works, but the Chuzzlewits were far from lovable. That he had something to say concerning the influence of selfishness, no one questioned, but the English people did not care to pay for so dour a sermon, nor the Americans for being scolded and ridiculed. The failure of *Chuzzlewit* to sell embarrassed him financially. He had established a scale of living on the luxurious basis provided by the royalties of *Pickwick.* He began to go deeper and deeper into debt. His publishers, apparently thinking that he had "shot his bolt," took advantage of a clause in their contract which further reduced his income.

The Christmas Carol. In this crisis he resolved to change his manner of living and to reduce his expenses. He planned to leave England and live upon the continent where living was cheaper. Before he went, however, he would make one last effort to re-woo Dame Fortune. In November of that year (1843) he brought forth his *Christmas Carol,* the first of a long line of annual Christmas books. It was a success from the very start. His best powers, his humor, his pathos, his bright poetic fancy, his kindly spirit—he gave them all free rein, and they made the little book one of the masterpieces of English literature. Dickens was the first English author to use children as his heroes and heroines. And he was the first author of any note to attempt to make his stories appeal to children. Tiny Tim, lovable, pathetic, and generous, captured everyone's heart.

Yet, popular as this book was, its sales were not sufficient to lift Dickens out of his debts which he describes as "terrific." He was now faced not with the advisability but with the necessity of drastic action. He broke with his old publishers, Chapman and Hall, and entered into a contract with another firm, Bradbury and Evans, who had once solicited his patronage and were still eager for it. They advanced him £2,800, which enabled him to pay some of his debts and to buy, as he said, " a good old shabby devil of a coach."

In an Old Coach to Italy. In this coach he packed his wife, his sister-in-law, the five Dickens children (the youngest only six months old), Roche, the man of all work, Anne, the maid, and two or three other servants and set out for France and Italy. Behind him he left his great house, his literary friends, and the maelstrom of social activities, public addresses, and parties, all of which he had loved but which he could no longer afford. He plunged, or rather (considering the character of the old coach) lumbered into the highways and byways of countries that were old in culture before

England was born. His good spirits did not fail him. He loved the gypsy life and regarded his multitudinous household as a continuous circus. He had been poor before and was not afraid to face poverty now, for he had confidence in his own developed powers of observation and expression.

When the old coach reached Genoa, Dickens found the city so much to his liking that he made it his Italian home. There he played as only Dickens could play when the printer was not calling for copy, and his expenses were not exceeding his income. He roamed all over the city. He fed upon the joyous spirit of its people and reveled in their romance.

The Chimes. One day the chimes of the many bells of Genoa's churches broke in upon him as he was cudgeling his brain for a subject for his next Christmas book which must be started, as it was already October. What should it be? Chimes! Yes, that was it! The bells suggested both the subject and the title of the book. He threw himself into it with all his heart and strength. He says: "All my affections and passions got twined and knotted up in it, and I became as haggard as a murderer long before I wrote 'The End.'" It is a story of toiling people, suffering, oppressed, and forgotten by the world but remembered by God. That is the keynote of the *Chimes*. In it he rang a bell in behalf of the poor and the downtrodden.

A Triumphal Return at Thirty-Two. When he had finished he determined to show the work to his old

79

cronies, and departed at once for a short visit to London. He made the trip in twenty-four days—fast time for an old coach—so eager was he to see his old friends. They assembled at Forster's house on December 2 to hear his story. Maclise, the artist, one of his intimate friends who was present, has bequeathed to us a priceless pencil drawing of that occasion. It shows among others Carlyle, Douglas Jerrold, Laman Blanchard, literary lights; Dyce Maclise and Stanfield, painters; and various other notables of the day. Dickens is portrayed as a kind of deity among them, a halo of light about his head, his hearers hanging on his every word. They laughed and cried as the story unfolded. And when it was finished they were, figuratively at least, at his feet. Dickens at thirty-two was now the undisputed prince of the story-tellers of his time.

Dombey and Son and David Copperfield. The flood-tide of his powers had only begun to roll in. Yet the rest of his story, even though it includes his most productive years, may be briefly told. He returned to Italy, toured it, came back to London, wrote *Pictures from Italy;* retreated to Switzerland; began *Dombey and Son* there; grew homesick and went back to his beloved London; wrote more of *Dombey and Son* and the whole of *The Battle of Life;* sojourned in Paris making friends with the elder Dumas and Victor Hugo; returned again to London and completed and published *Dombey and Son* and *David Copperfield.* Both proved hugh successes. He was now thirty-eight.

Hard Times. Then followed in steady succession *The Child's History of England,* the *Uncommercial Traveler,* and *Hard Times.* Few, if any, of his writings precipitated so much criticism and so much difference of opinion as *Hard Times.* Macaulay called it "sullen socialism" and could find himself in agreement with nothing Dickens said in it. John Ruskin approved, saying: "He is entirely right in his main drift and purpose in every book he has written; and all of them, but especially *Hard Times,* should be studied with close and earnest care by persons interested in social questions." Bernard Shaw insists that *Hard Times* is the really first great work of Dickens, the beginning of a "series of exposures of our civilization." Certainly Dickens had more in mind than just another story. He was concerned with the injustices of the social order and the sufferings of the poor. This concern had not been absent from his earlier works, but from now on it became increasingly manifest—the tragic note underneath his laughter. We shall hear more of it later.

Little Dorrit. Immediately after completing *Hard Times* he began *Little Dorrit.* While working on it he learned that Gad's Hill Place, the old mansion near his boyhood home, was for sale. He wanted it—this grand fairy castle of his childhood dreams. He could not afford it, but he must have it. So he bought it, and again plunged into debt. To pay it off he accelerated his already feverish pace of work. "I have no

81

relief but in action," he wrote. "I am incapable of rest. I am quite confident I should rust, break, and die if I spared myself. Much better to die doing." Harriet Martineau said: "I am much struck by his hysterical restlessness. It must be terribly wearing to his wife."

Failure in Domestic Adjustment. Possibly it was. And possibly, too, she was wearing upon him, for they were growing apart. "Poor Catherine and I are not made for each other, and there is no help for it," he wrote. "It is not only that she makes me uneasy and unhappy, but that I make her so too, and much more so. We are strangely ill-assorted for the bond there is between us. Her temperament will not go with mine." In May, 1858, they separated after living together twenty years and rearing six children. Dickens settled six hundred pounds a year on her. The eldest son, Charles, went with her. The other children and the aunt, Georgia Hogarth, remained with Dickens.

Public Readings. The joy he found in writing did not offset the maladjustment of his domestic relations. Nor did it satisfy either his energy or his debts. He began public readings of his works. Everywhere he was received with acclamation and he leaped again to the forefront of public attention as he journeyed throughout England, Scotland, and Ireland.

Tale of Two Cities. In the meantime, he had begun *The Tale of Two Cities* and somehow managed to keep the chapters going serially while he dashed about giving readings to great crowds. When he finished *The Tale of Two Cities* he began *Great Expectations* in the very next issue of the magazine. To most critics this book marks the height of his career as a novelist. He will still do *Our Mutual Friend* and various minor works. But he will never again equal the combination of character portrayal, dramatic intensity, humor, and tragedy of *Great Expectations*. The floodtide of his powers has reached its apogee.

At Forty-Eight. His public readings were bringing him such fame and profit that he threw all his failing strength into them. He was but forty-eight years of age, but already in the afternoon of his life and running almost breathlessly to a comparatively early sunset. Sorrows began to crowd upon him. His son, his good friend Thackeray, his business manager, and his brother-in-law all died within the space of a few months. But he pressed on without stopping. His left foot became infected and the shock of a railway accident impaired his nerves so that to ride upon a railroad train sometimes threw him into paroxysms of fear. To compensate for sorrow and sickness, he worked all the more strenuously. He seemed to defy the approaching end. His indomitable will and heroic struggle to keep going present a picture of pathos and grandeur. The story of his life, as Forster writes it, reads at this time like some ancient legend of an earthbound Prometheus defying the thunderbolts of Jove. He would rise from a sickbed to appear before an audience, finding in their applause better medicine than any doctor could give him. "The effect of the readings at Hastings and Dover," he wrote, "really seems to have outdone the best usual impression; and at Dover they would not go, but sat applauding like mad. . . . The people in the stalls set the example of laughing in the most curiously unreserved way; . . . the contagion extended to me, for one could not hear them without laughing too."

To America Again. America, forgetting his *American Notes* and *Chuzzlewit,* called him again. In the state of his health he should not have gone, but he wanted to see the country again, he wanted to drink at the well of American enthusiasm, and he needed American dollars. He was using little money for selfish pleasures these days. He knew that his strength was failing and he was thinking of the loved ones who were dependent upon him. Their care weighed upon him. He had been the mainstay of his parents in their declining years and of various other relatives who had never risen out of their want. Moreover, he wished to do for his children what had not been done for him—to leave them the wherewithal to face the world without the grinding poverty and tragedy which he had endured. The harvest of his years of sowing and labor must be garnered now or never.

So to America he came again. It was a triumphal procession through Boston, New Haven, Providence, Springfield, Worcester, New York, and Washington.

He was amazed not only at the prodigious changes in the size of the cities, but in their growth in culture. When he went to Washington President Johnson sent for him twice. In New York he had to give six farewells, so great were the crowds which insisted on hearing him.

Mounting Fame; Failing Strength. When he returned to England he kept up the furious pace and entered a contract to give a hundred public readings, for which he was to receive the unprecedented price of eight thousand pounds. He was suffering from his infected foot, from catarrh and insomnia, and paralysis was threatening. His physicians ordered him to rest. Instead he took on the additional labor of writing *The Mystery of Edwin Drood.* But no human being could stand such a strain. His health broke completely and he had to give up the public readings. He found compensation in the fact that Queen Victoria commanded him to visit her, which he did. It was the supreme honor in the life of the man who had once been a neglected child in London's slums.

His Last Request. He died suddenly on June 8, 1870, leaving *The Mystery of Edwin Drood* unfinished. His death brought grief to the humblest and the greatest homes in every civilized country. He was buried in the poets' corner of Westminster Abbey. The funeral was without pomp or ceremony, for in his will he had requested—

. . . . that I be buried in an inexpensive, unostenta-
tious, and strictly private manner; that no public an-
nouncement be made of the time or place of my burial;
that at the utmost not more than three plain mourn-
ing-coaches be employed; and that those who attend my
funeral wear no scarf, cloak, black bow, long hat-band,
or other revolting absurdity. I DIRECT that my
name be inscribed in plain English letters on my tomb,
without the addition of "Mr." or "Esquire." I con-
jure my friends on no account to make me the subject of any monument, memorial, or testimonial whatever. I rest my claims to the remembrance of my
country upon my published works, and to the remembrance of my friends upon their experience of me in
addition thereto. I commit my soul to the mercy of
God through our Lord and Saviour Jesus Christ, and I
exhort my dear children humbly to try to guide themselves by the teaching of the New Testament in its
broad spirit, and to put no faith in any man's narrow
construction of its letter here or there.[16]

The Life of Our Lord. So passed Charles Dickens.
In that will he epitomized the character he had been
growing these fifty-eight crowded years. Humble,
joyful, shunning cant and hating hypocrisy, he offered
no apology for the work to which he had given his
best labors, but directed his children to the book he
counted most valuable for their guidance through life
—the New Testament. He had so honored the New
Testament in his own home that he not only read
it to his children, but rewrote much of it in simple,

[16] Forster: *Op. cit.,* p. 671.

modern English so that they could understand it. That rewriting, which he entitled *The Life of Our Lord,* he never intended for publication, doubtless realizing his own lack of capacity to do its subject justice. But it is not without significance that when it was finally published in 1933 it became immediately a best seller and was syndicated in hundreds of newspapers throughout Great Britain and America, so that its actual number of readers probably exceeded any other of his works. Incidentally, the newspaper syndicate paid for this 14,000 word manuscript the highest price ever paid for any literary work—forty thousand pounds, or nearly $15 a word.

Since he rested his claims for remembrance upon his published works, together with the memories his friends had of him, and since we have dealt thus far primarily with the outward events of his life, it is pertinent now to ask, What memories of him are most worth cherishing? "The excellent," said Emerson, "as God lives, is permanent." What was most excellent in his life? Surely the answer has to do not with the amount of money he made or the miles he traveled, or the number of public readings he gave, or the quantity of books he published. It has to do rather with his purpose. with the quality of his inner life and of the books in which he expressed it, and with the sources of his power.

His Purpose. Was his purpose solely to enter-tain? That might have been enough, for God knows that burdened humanity needs entertainment. But he had a purpose far deeper. Unquestionably he did entertain. He made England and America laugh, but the laughter was not unmixed with tears, for along with the fun in his novels Dickens kept portraying the slums, the prisons, the poorhouses, the factories where children worked early and late, and the desperate living conditions of the lower classes. Just as Abraham Lincoln, when a young man, observed a Negro girl slave on an auction block being sold into slavery and resolved to "hit that thing hard" when he got a chance, so Dickens in the depths of his heart had determined to do what he could to make life less bitter for the poor from whose numbers he had risen. He deliberately made his stories serve this social and humanitarian purpose. He never forgot the ditch from which he had been digged. He was filled with pity especially for the children who had to live under the most degrading circumstances and who were doomed to a life of inequality and hardship. He would alleviate those hardships; he would do what he could to reform those conditions. In *David Copperfield* he enlightened the nation concerning what was going on in the slums and the terrible facts of juvenile delinquency and the adult exploitation of it. In *Nicholas Nickleby* he helped to mitigate the evils of private boarding schools. In *Oliver Twist* he revealed the conditions of the poor in English workhouses, victims of the social order suffering from injustices and lack of the necessities of life. In *Bleak*

House he called attention to the costly delays of the
law. In *Old Curiosity Shop* he attacked gambling. In
Little Dorrit he shamed his country for the persecution
of poor debtors.

Thus, underlying his laughter was Dickens' serious
purpose to make his novels instruments of reform. By
them he sought justice and social morality. His stories did more to correct social injustice than any other
effort of his age. Daniel Webster said that they did
more to ameliorate the condition of the English poor
than all the statesmen Great Britain had sent into Parliament. James T. Fields, in his *Yesterdays with Authors*,[17] wrote that even when Dickens was busiest with
his writings "he found opportunities of visiting personally those haunts of suffering in London which
needed the keen eye and sympathetic heart to bring them
before the public for relief. Whoever has accompanied
him, as I have, on his midnight walks into the cheap
lodginghouses provided for London's lowest poor, cannot have failed to learn lessons never to be forgotten.
Newgate and Smithfield were lifted out of their abom-
inations by his eloquent pen, and many a hospital is today all the better charity for having been visited and
watched by Charles Dickens. To use his own words,
through his whole life he did what he could to 'lighten
the lot of those rejected ones whom the world has too
long forgotten and too often misused.' "

[17] Page 249. Used by permission of, and by arrangement with,
Houghton Mifflin Company.

Robert Owen in the generation preceding Dickens had a like purpose, but chose a different method. Both men were equally passionate in their efforts in behalf of the common people. Both saw with clear vision the need of reforms in education, child labor, housing, prisons, factory life, and such. Both threw themselves with characteristic enthusiasm and energy into the battle for these reforms. Owen was probably more self-sacrificing and more indifferent to his own material interests. He made great social experiments in the hope of establishing a model community. But the fact remains that England knows and remembers Dickens with an affection far deeper than it extends to Robert Owen.

One cannot forego a reflection here upon the comparative effectiveness of the methods of art and sociology as used by these two great men. Both wanted to awaken the conscience of England. Dickens chose the indirect method of an art; Owen chose the direct method of sociology. Owen wrote no fiction. He "wasted" no time in description and narration. He preferred to marshal arguments, to convince by means of facts and figures, and to solve by means of practical experiments. His whole appeal was thus an appeal to reason, an appeal to the head. Dickens chose to appeal to the heart, to the feelings, the emotions, the motive power. His success is its own testimony of the relative power of the emotional approach in contrast to the intellectual, of the artist and the sociologist.

His Religion. His passion for helping the poor
did not come into existence by spontaneous combus-
tion. It seems to have sprung more naturally from religious roots. Deep in his heart was his belief in the
sacredness of human beings as children of a heavenly
Father. That belief is the central principle of the
Christian religion. Any social system, any institution
or national condition which oppressed human beings,
or in any way subtracted from their sacredness, was
therefore wrong. Here is the key for understanding
Dickens' hatred of slavery, of child labor, of debtors'
prison, of slums, of gin shops, of cruelty in every form.
Gilbert K. Chesterton saw truly when he said:

Dickens was sensitive, theatrical, amazing, a bit of a
dandy, a bit of a buffoon. . . . Yet it remains true that
he had in him a central part that was pleased only by
the most decent and the most reposeful rites, by things
of which the Anglican Prayer Book is most typical.[18]

This is not to say that Dickens was much of a church-
man. His devotion was to the broad spirit of the New
Testament rather than to the church whose broad lapses
from that spirit irked him. As a youth he had joined
the Church of England. But he often attacked it for
failing in its stewardship of Christian teaching and for
becoming so entangled in forms and catechisms that it
lost the essence of the gospel. Once in a moment of

[18] G. K. Chesterton: *Charles Dickens: A Critical Study*, pp. 221,
222. New York: Dodd, Mead & Co., 1906.

huff he became a Unitarian, but found that institution even less to his liking and soon returned to the Established Church.

No small part of his religion was his hatred of hypocrisy and intolerance. He denounced the "No Popery" riots in no uncertain terms:

Those shameful tumults, while they reflect indelible disgrace upon the time . . . and all who had act or part in them, teach a good lesson: that what we falsely call a religious cry is easily raised by men who have no religion and who in their daily practice set at naught the commonest principle of right and wrong; that it is begotten of intolerance and persecution: that it is senseless, besotted, inveterate, and unmerciful; all history teaches us.[19]

When he visited Avignon and saw the torture chamber in which the victims of the Inquisition had been made to suffer in the name of religion, he unleashed his powers of description.

Mash, mash, mash upon the sufferers' limbs.
See the stone trough! . . . For the water torture!
Gurgle, swill, bloat, burst, for the Redeemer's honour!
Suck the bloody rag deep down into your unbelieving body, heretic, at every breath you draw.
And when the executioner plucks it out reeking with the smaller mysteries of God's own image, know us for His chosen servants, true believers in the Sermon on the Mount, elect disciples of Him who never did a miracle

[19] Dickens, *Barnaby Rudge*, Preface.

92

but to heal; who never struck a man with palsy, blindness, deafness, drunkenness, madness, any one affliction of mankind! and never stretched His blessed hand out but to give relief.

ɪt aroused his indignation that the churches of his own day should give such little attention to matters of social justice—to slums, sweatshops, filthy factories, child labor—and so much to the outward show of religion. Against this outward show he used his genial satire and ridicule in nearly every one of his novels, especially in *Pickwick* and in *David Copperfield*. When *Pickwick* appeared in serial form this ridicule was taken too often as being directed against religion itself. In his preface to the papers when published in book form Dickens therefore wrote:

Lest there be those who do not perceive the difference between religion and cant, piety and pretense, a humble reverence for the truths of Scripture and an audacious and offensive obtrusion of its letter and not its spirit, let them understand it is always the latter and not the former that is satirized.

It is never out of season to protest against that familiarity with sacred things, or against that confounding of Christianity with any class of persons who have just enough religion to make them hate and not enough to make them love religion.[20]

But his most positive and personal statement of his own religious faith and practice he gave to his son

[20] Dickens: *Pickwick Papers*, Preface.

when the latter was leaving for Australia. Like most fathers, Dickens had found himself inarticulate in private conversation concerning the matters that were deepest in his heart. In this letter to his departing son he gave them expression and bared his own soul:

You will remember that at home you have never been harassed about religious observances or mere formalities, and I have always been anxious not to weary my children with such things before they were old enough to form opinions respecting them. You will therefore understand the better that I now most solemnly impress upon you the truth and beauty of the Christian religion as it came from Christ Himself, and the impossibility of your going far wrong if you humbly but heartily respect it.

Only one thing more on this head. The more we are in earnest as to feeling it, the less we are disposed to hold forth about it. *Never abandon the wholesome practice of saying your own private prayers night and morning. I have never abandoned it myself and I know the comfort of it.*[21]

His Sources of Power. The sources of Dickens' power, as near as we can appraise them from this brief study, lay in his determination to lift himself out of the slums, his unflagging industry, his sense of humor, his faculty for inventiveness, his vivid imagination, his unequaled skill in description, and above all his sincere championship of the weak and oppressed.

His sense of humor probably accounts for his mag-

[21] Forster: *Op. cit.,* p. 640.

nificent success in the delineation of character. He once wrote: "I have such an inexpressible enjoyment of what I see in a droll light that I dare say I pet it as if it were a spoiled child." Unquestionably it was this sense of humor which first gained for him the ear of England and America. Everybody wants to laugh. Most of us like to laugh at the foibles of others, and we can even smile at our own when we see them pictured good-naturedly as Dickens portrayed them.

His industry beggars all description. How any man could have written so much—and all by his own pen, never by dictation—in one lifetime must remain forever a mystery to those whose expression comes only with blood and sweat.

Whatever I have tried to do in life (he wrote, late in life), I have tried with all my heart to do well. What I have devoted myself to, I have devoted myself to completely. Never to put one hand to anything on which I could not throw my whole self, and never to affect depreciation of my work, whatever it was, I find now to have been my golden rules.[22]

His inventiveness seems to have been a native quality and never to have failed him, although it burned more brightly at some times than at others. Did it begin on that sickbed of his childhood when he was inventing stories and dramatizations in order to attract to his room the playmates he could not join out of doors?

[22] Forster: *Op. cit.*, p. 36.

His imagination was not unique in itself. The marvelous thing about it was the fact that he developed the ability to hold his mental images long enough and vividly enough in his mind to describe them on paper. Probably most of us have mental images so vivid that they arouse our emotions and call forth our deepest sympathies, but they take the wings of the morning and disappear beyond the horizon while we are still looking for our pencils. Dickens somehow managed to harness his images to his pen. He drew every character, every scene with such minute care and accuracy that the reader had the convincing impression of reality. His descriptive faculty he had cultivated as a child and again as a reporter. Doubtless his rapid shorthand helped him to etch into his mind by way of his fingers the scenes he wished to imprison in words. Those scenes were by no means limited to his fancies. Everything he saw and experienced was grist for his mill. He took the situations, the characters, the flavor of everyday life and wove them into his stories. He seized upon every dramatic possibility, every peculiarity of voice and manner, every unusual physical feature or social custom and built them into his novels. Thus when people read them they felt they were reading their own lives retold to them.

His sympathy came out of his long suffering. He felt and understood the tragedies and comedies of the poor because he had lived them himself.

His passion for helping the weak and oppressed lifted

his writings out of the commonplace category of mere entertainment and imparted to them a quality that will make them endure as long as human beings struggle against poverty and social injustice.

By the power drawn from such sources he fulfilled his cherished purpose to "leave his hand upon the time, lastingly upon the time, with one tender touch for the mass of toiling people that nothing could obliterate."

MATTHEW ARNOLD

1822-1888

MATTHEW ARNOLD was not dramatic. To look at him, a mild-mannered, squeaky-voiced Englishman with mutton-chop whiskers, high stiff collar, Ascot tie, cutaway coat, striped trousers, spats, and square-toed shoes, no one would ever suspect him of power. He would be suspected of nothing better or worse than monotony. As a matter of fact, his life had a deal of desert monotony in it. But in a collection of biographies where most of the subjects are electric, there ought to be place for one quiet soul who made a dent in the world in spite of his mild-mannered, unexciting, monotonous personality.

His story is the simple story of a cultured man. It contains no sensations, no battles, no campaigns, no crises, no great honors, no blood, no thunder. This man never did anything more exciting than inspect secondary schools, lecture to American audiences, teach poetry, write books, and go fishing. Cultural history on the surface always seems dull. But underneath the surface flows silently the deep, strong current—the real history of human achievement. In that current Matthew Arnold lived and slowly but surely he influenced its direction.

The Times. That current came out of the eighteenth century, its waters still seething and bloody with revolution. America and France had violently thrown off the yoke of political tyranny. Thrones were falling and new states rising under the leadership of Metternich, Cavour, and Bismarck. England under the guidance of Gladstone and Disraeli had managed to steer clear of the more violent political storms on the continent and was now pushing her empire eastward and southward.

Meanwhile, the industrial revolution had stirred up even greater turmoil. Power looms had replaced hand labor in homes. Inventors had discovered the motive power of steam, and steamship and railroads hurried raw materials to the growing cities and manufactured products to the provinces. Factories sprang up where women and children worked long hours for low wages. Around the factories slums appeared in which poverty-ridden workers by the tens of thousands lived in filthy tenements along narrow, muddy streets and stinking alleys. The east end of London stood in black contrast to the magnificence of the royal court. The power of the old aristocracy dwindled steadily. Between the many poor and the few rich the middle class began to exercise increasing power and to make demands. The aristocracy gave way to these demands and through the reform bill of 1832 granted wide suffrage. The middle class thus gained the balance of power and really ruled England.

Still greater conflicts disturbed the philosophical and religious life of the times. Old authorities crumbled and no new ones took their place. The churches which had felt the impact of the Wesleyan revival in the eighteenth century now in the nineteenth had the very foundations of their faith challenged by the Higher Criticism of the Bible and by the implications of the evolutionary theories of a young scientist named Charles Darwin. Huxley and Spencer threw their weight on the side of Darwin and the long struggle for reconstruction in religion began. No one has described that struggle and its accompanying upheaval better than Arnold himself, who viewing it wrote in his *Bacchanalia:*

> Thundering and bursting
> In torrents, in waves,
> Carolling and shouting
> Over tombs, amid graves,
> See! On the cumbered plain
> Clearing a stage,
> Scattering the past about
> Comes the new age.[1]

All this confusion and conflict and questioning of authority had its inevitable effect in a letdown of moral standards. What was right and what was wrong? What was most worth giving one's life for? The pas-

---

[1] *Arnold's Poetical Works.* The Macmillan Company. Used by permission.

sionate enthusiasm for political liberty which Keats and Shelley had voiced meant little to the ever-increasing multitude of factory workers. The measured eloquence of Browning and Tennyson in praise of individualistic righteousness meant even less. The urban mind unable or unwilling to think through a new social ethic sought escape in a craving for sensation and scandal—a craving to which the newspapers pandered.

Into such times in the year 1822 Matthew Arnold was born on Christmas Eve at Laleham near Staines, England. He was "brought up and reared in hours of change, alarm, surprise." Yet his immediate environment was not one of "alarm and surprise," but the peaceful life of a quiet English countryside. He was never to enter the conflicts of his day with a sword. He chose the humbler weapon—a pen.

Heredity. Arnold's complex personality and breadth of mind can be understood only as it is recognized that two great cultural streams flowed into his life. One stream of culture stressed conduct and obedience, energy and strength as the chief virtues. He called this stream Hebraism because these are the virtues the English absorbed from the Bible. The other stream of culture stressed seeing things as they are, intelligence, spontaneity of consciousness. He called this stream Hellenism because these were the virtues the English absorbed from the ancient Greeks. These streams converged upon young Matthew in his home, and later in Oxford.

His Father. His father, Dr. Thomas Arnold, mediated the Hebraic tradition to him. England had one of its greatest educators in Dr. Arnold, headmaster of Rugby. He contributed an intelligent liberalism to educational practice by his administration of the famous school. Under his direction Rugby became a place where boys learned fundamental lessons of self-government and self-discipline as well as classical languages. A profound recognition of the necessity for right decisions in the moral issues of life undergirded Dr. Arnold's progressive development of educational method. He maintained at all times his deep and sincere religious devotion. Matthew never forgot the debt which he owed to his father for this religious and moral heritage. Dr. Arnold died when the boy was twenty years old. In *Rugby Chapel* Matthew has made imperishable the memory of the great headmaster:

Fifteen years have gone round
Since thou arosest to tread,
In the summer morning, the road
Of death, at a call unforeseen,
Sudden. For fifteen years,
We who till then in thy shade
Rested as under the boughs
Of a mighty oak, have endured
Sunshine and rain as we might,
Bare, unshaded, alone,
Lacking the shelter of thee.

Yet, in some far-shining sphere,
Conscious or not of the past,
Still thou performest the word

Of the Spirit in whom thou dost live,
Prompt, unwearied, as here.
Still thou upraisest with zeal
The humble good from the ground,
Sternly repressest the bad;
Still, like a trumpet, dost rouse
Those who with half-open eyes
Tread the border-land dim
'Twixt vice and virtue; reviv'st,
Succorest. This was thy work,
This was thy life upon earth.[2]

His Mother and Home. Mary Penrose Arnold, Matthew's mother, was intelligent, witty, sympathetic, strong of character. His letters to her reveal tenderness and great depth of feeling in their relationship. The nine children in the Arnold home inherited a tradition of learning. Teaching had constituted the principal vocation of the family for many generations. The children had the challenge and the opportunity to know the best that the world's great minds and spirits had produced. Family ties of love and devotion fostered the development of poised personalities.

Dr. Arnold disliked the landscape around Rugby. He thought it offered too little beauty to his family. He moved them, therefore, to a country home near Foxhow. Here natural beauty kindled the spirit and shed its gracious light upon the growing, sensitive boy. Here also he felt the influence of that high-souled interpreter of nature, Wordsworth.

[2] *Op. cit.* Used by permission.

Rugby. Matthew's early education was in the hands of his uncle, the Rev. John Buckland, who conducted a private school. Later he went to Winchester, and at the age of fifteen entered Rugby where he found a combination of strict discipline, classical studies, and progressive educational methods. Here particularly the Hebraic tradition made an indelible impression upon him.

Oxford. The attainment of a Balliol scholarship enabled him to go to Oxford. His father did not readily consent, however. He objected strenuously to the Catholic revival that was then in progress at the university. He eventually yielded, remarking that at least at Oxford "a man was made master of three or four great books for life," and among them Aristotle. So Matthew went to Oxford. He absorbed Aristotle. The Greek spirit, the love of beauty, the pursuit of the harmonious, perfectly developed life, more and more took possession of him. With simple eloquence he expresses the love for Oxford which remained always one of the deepest sentiments of his life:

Steeped in sentiment she lies, spreading her gardens to the moonlight, and whispering from her towers the last enchantments of the Middle Age, who will deny that Oxford, by her ineffable charm, keeps ever calling us nearer to the true goal of all of us, to the ideal, to perfection, to beauty, in a word, which is only truth seen from another side.[3]

[3] Herbert W. Paul: *Matthew Arnold,* p. 75. New York: The Macmillan Company, 1925.

At Oxford sweet reasonableness tempered puritan moralism, but received from the latter direction and firmness.

There he came to know and love great personalities. Among the older men, Cardinal Newman's profound and mystical piety formed a sharp contrast to the refined and cultured scholarship of Jowett. Among his personal friends the closest were John Duke Cleriedge, afterwards Lord Chief Justice of England, and John Campbell Shairp, principal of the United Colleges of Saint Andrews. He felt the deepest attachment to Arthur Hugh Clough, whose tragic death he mourned in his poem *Thyrsis*. The memory of the friendships of those college days remained one of the lasting joys of his life.

At twenty-one, while still at Oxford, he won the Newdigate prize with a poem on Cromwell. At twenty-three he was elected a Fellow of Oriel College. Upon leaving college he became assistant headmaster of Rugby for two years. At twenty-five he resigned this position to become private secretary to Lord Lansdowne, an eminent liberal statesman, a position which plunged him at once into the turbulent flood of politics.

Politics and Poetry. Terrific struggles were engaging the French and Germans as well as the English. The French were bringing forth the Second Republic and baptizing it in blood. The Germans were having some abortive revolts along the Rhine. The English were rioting over Chartism. And everywhere the industrial

105

revolution with its new inventions and machines, its factories and slums, was complicating the business of daily life for the humblest and the greatest. Nowhere was security, nowhere peace. Even in religion the foundations crumbled, for were not the higher critics and the Darwinians blasting at the Rock of Ages? So at least it seemed to many. A mood of bitterness and despair took possession of men's minds.

Then Matthew Arnold picked up his pen and began to write. And to write—of all things—poetry. This was no time for poetry. The hour demanded action. Everyone said so. But Arnold thought there was too much action. A little meditation might help, a little brooding before more bloodshed. So at twenty-seven he wrote *The Strayed Reveller* and *Empedocles on Etna*. No one paid any attention. The books failed. Thereupon he selected the best from these two, added *Sohrab and Rustum* and *The Scholar Gipsy* and thus produced a third book. This one caught on, probably because of the great dramatic power of *Sohrab and Rustum,* and he followed it with a fourth, *Poems, Second Series,* which made such an impression that he was invited two years later to the Chair of Poetry in Oxford. It was only a part-time position, requiring half a dozen lectures a year, but it gave him prestige.

"During his occupancy of the Chair," says Williams S. Knickerbocker, "he laid the foundations of his fame as one of the most significant literary critics by learning the fundamental lesson which any critic of permanent significance must learn—the lesson of detachment, of subordination of self, of renouncement." [4] That trait stands out in all his after-writings: *he subordinates himself*. In fact, self-subordination became such a characteristic of him that he requested before his death that no formal biography of him ever be written, a request that has made difficult the accumulation of material even for so short a sketch as this. He felt that *he* was not important; what counted was the light that filtered through his mind. It was the light; not the filter.

Growing Purpose. Now that he had a toe-hold in the realm of scholarship he decided to climb out of the whirlpool of politics. He would think while the rest of the populace fought. He would think not about himself but about them and how to save them from so much misery. In place of their bitterness he would endeavor to bring reasonableness, sweetness. In place of their dark despair he would bring light and hope. He wrote to his mother his intention "to come out from time to time as the organ of the body of quiet and reasonable people; to be of use in the troubled times which are before us as a healing and a reconciling influence." In his *Thyrsis*, where he mourned the tragic death of his friend Arthur Hugh Clough, he put the same purpose in poetic form:

* From the Introduction to *Culture and Anarchy*, p. xi. Modern Readers' Series. Macmillan, 1925. Used by permission.

A fugitive and gracious light he seeks,
  Shy to illumine; and I seek it too.
    This does not come with houses or with gold,
    With place, with honor, and a flattering crew;
      'Tis not in the world's market bought and sold:
        But the smooth-slipping weeks
      Drop by, and leave its seeker still untired;
        Out of the heed of mortals he is gone,
        He wends unfollowed, he must house alone;
      Yet on he fares, by his own heart inspired.[5]

Bread and Butter and Marriage. It's all very well, says the practical man, to have such notions about the way to use one's life, but how about bread and butter? Will the fellows in the hurly-burly of the scramble of life pay anybody for sitting on the sidelines and having noble thoughts? Young Matthew Arnold had no delusions on that point. He didn't expect pay. To earn his bread and butter he secured an appointment as inspector of secondary schools. Next, he married Miss Frances Lucy Wightman, daughter of an English judge. Then, his home established, he settled down to a *thirty-five-year stretch of inspecting schools in day-times, lecturing occasionally at Oxford, and devoting his spare hours to interpreting and influencing the whirling life around him through poems and essays—to bringing sweetness and light in the place of bitterness and despair.*

It sounds easy enough, simple enough, writing it that way. But it wasn't quite so easy. The inspection job

[5] *Arnold's Poetical Works.* The Macmillan Company. Used by permission.

108

was a grind in itself, and he did not neglect it. One writer, speaking of Arnold's studies of secondary schools and the recommendations that came out of them, said:

Of all the educational reformers in the last century, not excepting his father, Mr. Arnold was the most enlightened, the most far-sighted, the most fair-minded.[6]

The irksome task of inspection and report-writing took time and energy which might have been spent upon poetry and essays for the good of the world. In one letter he spoke of writing reports until his fingers ached, and exclaimed:

After all it is absurd that all the best of my days should be taken up with matter which thousands of other people could do just as well as I; and that what I have a special turn for doing I should have no time for.[7]

In another note he frankly confessed his inability to examine little girls in needlework! Yet economic necessity kept him at the report-making job for thirty-five years.

It did drain his energy and sapped some of his creative urge, but he marshaled what was left and the poems and essays flowed steadily from his pen. His spirit shines through these lines, perhaps written while his fingers still ached from the reports:

[6] Herbert W. Paul: *Op. cit.,* p 112.
[7] *Letters,* Vol. 2, p. 50.

Most men in a brazen prison live,
Where, in the sun's hot eye,
With heads bent o'er their toil, they languidly
Their lives to some unmeaning task-work give,
Dreaming of nought beyond their prison-wall.

. . . . *

And the rest, a few,
Escape their prison, and depart
On the wide ocean of life anew.[8]

Arnold was one who escaped the prison of a routine grind and departed "on the wide ocean of life anew" with his creative writing.

Moreover, the routine grind gave him a steady contact with reality. It kept his feet on the ground. On one occasion especially it gave impetus and direction to his writing. He had been assigned to study certain schools and universities on the Continent. The assignment gave him the opportunity to meet and talk with many of the leading French and German educators, statesmen, and writers. He interviewed them not only about schools but about the trends of social and political thought. He came back with his head full of new ideas about democracies and the dangers in them and around them. And then he began to write a new series of essays warning his readers of those dangers and pointing a way out.

* From *A Summer Night*. *Arnold's Poetical Works*, p. 166. Published by the Macmillan Company. Used by permission.

Culture as Medicine. In that series he held that the medicine the sick democracies needed was culture, which he defined as "contact with the best that has been thought and said in the world." They were living too much in the present and with too little regard for the social and spiritual history of mankind. A treatment of culture would produce intelligence, patience, a new sense of perspective. He devoted his next lectures at Oxford to this subject, comparing the national character of the English, the French, and the Germans and tracing their respective roots. It was not altogether a popular thing to do, for his countrymen did not always shine in the comparison. But it made them think. It cooled their national self-love somewhat and made them a little more humble. And it started Arnold upon a line of thought which was to culminate some years later in his great book, *Culture and Anarchy.*

Thus this quiet scholar quietly lived and quietly grew. Thus he began to have a greater and greater influence upon the minds of his fellow men. He received little support and less encouragement from the "practical" statesmen of the day. The liberals complained that he wouldn't help their programs of immediate *action.* The newspapers would have none of his culture. They knew what the public wanted and they would give it what it wanted. Sensation and scandal —that was the formula. Arnold saw their shortsightedness and flayed it. "By shooting all this garbage on your public," he wrote, "you are preparing and assuring for your English people an immorality as deep and as wide as that which destroys the Latin nations." [9]

Steadily, quietly, insistently he kept on, year after year. Never rich, never popular. He worked like leaven in the body politic. He was in no hurry. The world would not be saved in a day. It would not be saved at all until intelligence and morality had their say. And that would be only when men stopped fighting and began to meditate upon the meaning and the purpose and the true way of life. In every book that he wrote he had a definite point to make, a point that brought him a step closer to his goal of transforming the bitterness and darkness of his time to sweetness and light. He had begun in the field of literature and gradually expanded into the fields of politics and religion.

In his *Essays on Criticism*—a work which has become a classic in its field—he sought sounder principles of literary criticism. The romanticists of the day had swung so far away from the traditional criteria that few, if any, standards remained. Arnold reintroduced responsibility into criticism, holding that the critic must have not only a point of departure, but an ideal. He stated the ideal and the principles of criticism so thoroughly that, as one writer said, "to read them qualified one to be a critic." This was an overstatement, but a significant tribute. In *Culture and Anarchy* he turned the searchlight of his thought on the political movements

[9] G. W. E. Russell: *Matthew Arnold*, p. 99.

of his day and, as we shall see presently, pointed the way by which modern states might steer clear of the rocks of anarchy. In *Literature and Dogma* Arnold threw down the challenge squarely and clearly to the old theological authorities. Anyone who wishes to sense the spirit and meaning of the liberalization of Christian theology need read nothing more than this essay. There he may find the whole story told in matchless English prose. The book ranked Arnold as one of the great liberators of the human spirit from the dogmas of outworn theology.

A homely illustration may make clearer just what Arnold was doing in this sort of writing. Imagine an old-time auto race with three or four "gasoline buggies" bumping along a dusty highroad, rattling, knocking, and steaming as their drivers pushed their crude machines to the limit and sought to take every advantage fair or foul that would put them ahead. The crowd on the sidelines would become immensely partisan and shout cheers for their favorites and jeers at the others. The true engineer, however, would quietly watch the performance of the respective cars, then go back to his laboratory and bend his head over new drawings of improved motors, frames, wheels. By and by he would come out with a better model. Thus Arnold watched the great social machines of his day, the schools, the state, the press, and the churches, and like an engineer went into his study to reflect upon them, criticize them, and suggest new designs.

Take his *Culture and Anarchy* as an example. We
have seen how old thrones were falling and young
democracies were taking their place. But the young
democracies were having their troubles. They were
functioning very badly, steaming and clattering. The
majority of the people were shouting and fighting about
them. Arnold reflected. And this was the gist of his
reflection: Democracies tend inevitably toward anarchy
unless they are permeated by ideals of perfection of individuals and of state. *Culture is the study of and
effort toward these ideals of perfection.* It includes a
cultivation of art, science, poetry, philosophy, and religion. The churches are saying that what man needs is
religion. But religion alone is not enough, for religion
aims at perfection of human nature only on its moral
side, whereas culture aims at perfection of human nature on all its sides. Culture is possessed by the scientific passion as well as by the passion for doing good.
Religion without culture is inadequate. It is quite too
apt to go off into fanaticism or bigotry or works of
zealous ignorance. Intelligence and beauty must enter
into any ideal of perfection before the fervor of religion
can become thoroughly effective. "The great men of
culture are those who have had a passion for dif-
fusing, for making prevail the best knowledge, the
best ideas of their time." Let us as a nation give our
attention to producing such men. Let us hold before
their minds not simply the dream of personal freedom
but the dream of an ideal State. Let us entrust that

114

ideal State with stringent powers for the general advantage and for controlling individual wills in the name of an interest wider than that of individuals. Let us make it the organ of our collective best self. Such a State will not be in danger of anarchy, for it will rest upon the solid rocks of intelligence and righteousness.

So brief a summary necessarily omits his specific applications to the institutions of his day. The whole argument sounds fairly familiar today. But in the 1870's it was strange doctrine. The English people were not thinking of the ideal State. They were taking pride in their large families and just beginning that worship of bigness, speed, and external show which characterized so large a proportion of the Western world a generation ago. Arnold applied his thought to such popular ideas and showed up their essential nonsense. Here is a typical shaft:

Population again, and bodily health and vigor are things which are nowhere treated in such an unintelligent, misleading, exaggerated way as in England. . . . Why one has heard people . . . who would talk of our large English families in quite a solemn strain, as if they had something in itself beautiful, elevating, and meritorious in them; as if the British Philistine would have only to present himself before the Great Judge with his twelve children in order to be received among the sheep as a matter of right. [10]

He went on to contrast the conditions of the children

[10] Arnold: *Culture and Anarchy,* p. 48. Published by the Macmillan Company. Used by permission.

of London's slums with the condition of children in a well-ordered, intelligently administered state, where all would have an opportunity to develop normally. He thus endeavored to plant in the popular imagination the picture of an ideal State instead of the ideal of raising families of twelve children!

His American Tour. Naturally the young democracies resented such sharp criticism of their expanding egos. They called him a radical! But they knew he was saying things they ought to hear. And his ideas about perfected individuals and a perfected state appealed to their own youthful idealism. Leaders of American thought invited him to come to their shores and lecture. He came. His lecture tour of the United States in 1884 presented the picture of a sensitive scholar in clear relief against the background of America of the gilded age.

His own account of the journey as found in his letters moves one alternately to amusement and sympathy. The letter written just before Arnold arrived in New York flows along in his usual tranquil vein. But in the first letter written after the arrival all tranquility has fled:

On Monday morning we landed and ever since I have been in a whirl, hardly able to do more writing than the signing of my name, the demand for my autograph being incessant. . . . The blaring publicity of this place is beyond all that I had any idea of. [11]

[11] *Letters*, Vol. II, pp. 257, 258.

And again, "The newspapers make life terrible." The
Chicago *Tribune* attacked him for lecturing for money.
He later declared that the best part of getting back to
England would be that he would no longer have to read
the American papers. He felt that the love of quiet
and dislike of the crowd had gone out of American
life entirely, and thanked heaven that America only
confirmed him in his desire to seek the secluded life as
much as possible.

The lecture tour achieved success, though Arnold
was really not a good lecturer, finding it difficult to
make his rather thin and high-pitched voice audible.
People came to hear him, but his tour was no triumphal
procession, as Dickens' had been. The complacent op-
timism of young America found Arnold's clear analysis
of democratic institutions too strong meat. Here is
a taste of it as he gave it to them in his lecture, *Numbers; or, the Majority and the Remnant.* It differed
strikingly from the spread-eagle, flag-waving oratory
so current in that day.

In these United States you are fifty millions and
more. I suppose that, as in England, as in France, as
everywhere else, so likewise here, the majority of the
people doubt very much whether the majority is unsound; or, rather, they have no doubt at all about the
matter—they are sure that it is not unsound. But let
us consent tonight to remain to the end in the ideas of
the sages and prophets whom we have been following
all along, and let us suppose that in the present actual
stage of the world, as in all the stages through which

the world has past hitherto, the majority be in general
unsound everywhere. Where is the failure? I suppose
that in a democratic community like this—with its new-
ness, its magnitude, its strength, its life of business, its
sheer freedom and equality—the danger is in the absence of the discipline of respect; in hardness and ma-
terialism, exaggeration and boastfulness; in a false
smartness, a false audacity, a want of soul and deli-
cacy. "Whatsoever things are *elevated*"—Whatsoever
things are noble, serious, have true elevation—that,
perhaps in our mind, is the maxim which points to
where the failure of the unsound majority, in a great
democracy like yours, will probably lie. At any rate,
let us for the moment agree to suppose so. And the
philosophers and the prophets—whom I at any rate am
disposed to believe—and who say that moral causes
govern the standing and the falling of states, will tell
us that the failure to mind whatsoever things are elevated must impair with an inexorable fatality the life
of a nation, just as the failure to mind whatsoever
things are just, or whatsoever things are pure, will
impair it; and that if the failure to mind whatsoever
things are elevated should be real in your American
democracy, and should grow into a disease, and take
firm hold on you, then the life of even these great
United States must inevitably be impaired more and
more until it perish.

Then from this hard doctrine we will betake ourselves to the more comfortable doctrine of *the remnant*.
"The remnant shall return;" shall convert and be healed
itself first, and shall then recover the unsound majority.[13]

[13] Matthew Arnold: *Discourses in America*, pp. 64-68. Published
by the Macmillan Company. Used by permission.

This gospel of the remnant was harsh doctrine to those who were worshiping majorities. Yet no one arose to answer him.

His Personality. This brings us to the question: What sort of personality had this quiet scholar been growing underneath his correct English waistcoat that he could be so irreverent about majorities? Quiet though he was, he was certainly no "softie," if one may use an expressive bit of American slang. He was genial, friendly, clever, lovable, generous, interested in all human life. He liked the out-of-doors and vigorous sports. He thought fishing too tame, but in his later years enjoyed it more and more. He had a genius for friendships. He maintained a spirit of modesty and generosity in the face of the criticisms hurled against him. In *Culture and Anarchy* he used himself as an example of the defects of the middle class.

His personality shines through his letters and his poems more clearly than any of his other writings. His letters are simple, beautifully phrased, above all, human. He wrote not only of books and politics and religion, but of cricket matches, apricot trees in full bloom, a friend's pigs, the city parks, the hay harvest (and, incidentally, about hay fever), holly and fir trees, daffodils, lovely women, the death of a favorite pony, a clump of blue violets.

His Poetry. In his poetry he appears not as the stern moralist or the critic of social institutions, but as an artist. He had a rare gift for the simple, unaffected

delineation of a spiritual mood and the expression of a
philosophic insight. His *East London* contains a whole
philosophy of life in a few clear-cut lines:

'Twas August, and the fierce sun overhead
Smote on the squalid streets of Bethnal Green,
And the pale weaver, through his windows seen
In Spitalfields, look'd thrice dispirited.

I met a preacher there I knew, and said:
"Ill and o'erwork'd, how fare you in this scene?"
"Bravely!" said he; "for I of late have been
Much cheer'd with thoughts of Christ, *the living bread.*"

O human soul! as long as thou canst so
Set up a mark of everlasting light,
Above the howling senses' ebb and flow,

To cheer thee, and to right thee if thou roam,
Not with lost toil thou labourest through the night!
Thou mak'st the heaven thou hop'st indeed thy home.[13]

His *Sohrab and Rustum* reveals his deep sense of
the tragic in human life. In heroic style reminiscent
of the Greek tragedies, Arnold in this poem tells the
story of the Persian warrior Rustum who unwittingly
slew his own son in a mighty duel. It is too long to
quote here, but this sketch of Arnold's life will not
have been written in vain if it introduces some new
reader to the simple yet powerful epic told in flawless
rhythm and perfect diction.

[13] *Arnold's Poetical Works*. The Macmillan Company. Used by
permission.

His *Dover Beach* conveys something of this same
sense of the tragic in life, a sense which deepened in
him after the early death of his two sons:

The sea is calm tonight.
The tide is full, the moon lies fair
Upon the straits; on the French coast, the light
Gleams and is gone; the cliffs of England stand,
Glimmering and vast, out in the tranquil bay.
Come to the window, sweet is the night air!
Only, from the long line of spray
Where the sea meets the moon-blanch'd sand,
Listen! you hear the grating roar
Of pebbles which the waves draw back, and fling,
At their return, up the high strand,
Begin and cease, and then again begin,
With tremendous cadence slow, and bring
The eternal note of sadness in.

Sophocles long ago
Heard it on the Aegean, and it brought
Into his mind the turbid ebb and flow
Of human misery: we
Find also in the sound a thought,
Hearing it by this distant northern sea.

The sea of faith
Was once, too, at the full, and round earth's shore
Lay like the folds of a bright girdle furl'd.
But now I only hear
Its melancholy, long, withdrawing roar,
Retreating, to the breath
Of the night-wind, down the vast edges drear
And naked shingles of the world.

Ah, love, let us be true
To one another! for the world, which seems
To lie before us like a land of dreams,
So various, so beautiful, so new,
Hath really neither joy, nor love, nor light,
Nor certitude, nor peace, nor help for pain;
And we are here as on a darkling plain
Swept with confused alarms of struggle and flight,
Where ignorant armies clash by night.[14]

His Sources of Power. The religion of this man
was the force which bound his capacities together and
gave them impetus, direction, and power. God to him
was "that power outside of ourselves which makes for
righteousness." He was an active force in the universe.
Man's duty consists in conforming his own wishes and
desires to the ideal of righteousness toward which God
works. God works in human life, leading it in His
own good time to a higher level. In his poem *Kensing-
ton Gardens,* in lines reminiscent of Wordsworth's
Tintern Abbey, Arnold expressed this sense of the divine in life:

Calm soul of all things! make it mine
To feel, amid the city's jar,
That there abides a peace of thine,
Man did not make, and cannot mar.

Again in *Morality* he sensed the enveloping mystery in
which man lives and moves:

[14] *Op. cit.*

122

We cannot kindle when we will
 The fire that in the heart resides;
The spirit bloweth and is still,
 In mystery our soul abides.
But tasks in hours of insight will'd
Can be through hours of gloom fulfill'd.[15]

Holding this simple, humble belief in God, Arnold was yet not orthodox. He attacked with great vigor the pretentious mass of dogmas upon which the various churches insisted. He had little patience with what he called "our mechanical and materialistic theology with its insane license of affirmation about God; its insane license of affirmation about a future state." [16] He found in all such theology "really the secret of the poverty and inanition of our faith."

He was a member of the Anglican Church not only because he had been brought up within it, but also because he believed that in its Christian-Hebrew tradition the accumulated religious experience of the past made the supreme contribution to the enrichment of life in the present. He was convinced that as men grew more intelligent in religion they would despise the narrowness and conflicts and divisiveness of religious sects. Protestants he held would be better off within the Anglican fold, and he looked forward to the religion of the future as a transformed Catholicism.

His religious faith was not only a dynamic for his

[15] *Op. cit.*
[16] *Culture and Anarchy*, p. 19. Published by the Macmillan Company.

life but a guide in private and social morality toward the perfection which he thought the ultimate goal of human effort. He once defined religion as "morality tinged by emotion." He insisted that religion demands "a serious attending to righteousness and dwelling upon it." [17] The moral experience, he said, lies at the heart of religion.

The first man who was thrilled with gratitude, devotion, and the sense of joy and peace not of his own making which followed the exercise of self-control, had religion revealed to him.[18]

He held that this experience is not restricted to a few elect souls, but is the common property of every man, wise or simple, who strives toward goodness.

This combination of religious faith, moral earnestness, and pursuit of perfection required self-discipline. He was willing to pay the price. He accepted the discipline not as penance, but as something that ennobled life.

To walk staunchly in the best light, to be strait and sincere with oneself, not to be of the number of those who say and do not, to be in earnest—this is the discipline by which alone man is enabled to secure his life from thraldom to the passing moment, and to his bodily senses, to ennoble it and to make it Eternal.

Self-discipline of this sort made it possible for him

[17] *Literature and Dogma*, p. 17.
[18] *Ibid.*, p. 44.

to appropriate the best of the past. Humbly, patiently, he disciplined his naturally fine mind and body to conform to the best ideals he knew. His sweetness of temper and sense of humor prevented his self-discipline from making him crabbed. His human sympathy kept him kindly and tolerant of the failings of others.

Thus we see this quiet scholar taking pains with his own character. He applied to himself his counsels of perfection. For from the time he left Oxford to his quiet death in 1888 he sought to develop his own excellence, not to make a splurge of it, not to make a fortune by it, but to influence by it the deep currents of thought and feeling that were carrying in their stream the ultimate destinies of his fellow men. The culture he had acquired from his great father and his intelligent, sympathetic mother, from the Jewish-Christian tradition of energetic righteousness, and from the Hellenistic atmosphere and study in Rugby and Oxford —all this culture he distilled in the alembic of his own soul before he preached it to the world. In that fact lay one of the deepest sources of his power. He would have been the first to insist that he did not achieve perfection. But culture is the *pursuit* of perfection, not its achievement. And he pursued it with diligence and with self-denial.

How much power did Arnold have? Did he really accomplish anything permanent? A half century has passed since he died. New wars impend. Anarchy

again seems just around the corner. In our chaotic
life "with its sick hurry, its divided aims," we who

> See all the sights from pole to pole
> And glance and nod and bustle by
> And never once possess our soul
> Before we die—

we yet hear the gentle whisper of Matthew Arnold
like the still small voice of conscience after the earth-
quake, wind, and fire. But the whisper annoys us. It
is too gentle. Not enough action in it. We know very
well that the quiet voice of culture cannot save our
world or make a new one. It takes more than education
to do that. Men are too selfish—we know that. They
must be coerced, legislated, compelled by force. Arnold,
you are too meek, we won't listen—

But from somewhere out of the darkness and across
the years comes an echo of an answer he once made
when men of his own day derided him and other Oxford scholars for their gentle ways:

I am all in the faith and tradition of Oxford. I say
boldly that this our sentiment for beauty and sweetness, our sentiment against hideousness and rawness,
has been at the bottom of our attachment to so many
beaten causes, of our opposition to so many triumphant
movements. And the sentiment is true, and has never
been wholly defeated, and has shown its power even in
its defeat. We have not won our political battles, we
have not carried our main points, we have not stopped
our adversaries' advance, we have not marched vic-
toriously with the modern world; but *we have told*

silently upon the mind of the country, we have pre-
pared currents of feeling which sap our adversaries'
position when it seems gained, we have kept up our own
communications with the future.[19]   (Italics ours.)

H. G. Wells said the other day that if we had listened
to Matthew Arnold a generation ago we might have
avoided the World War.   When the tumult and shouting of our own day have subsided we may again hear his
voice pleading for the pursuit of culture—a culture that
combines righteousness and intelligence—and we may
listen.   For Matthew Arnold still keeps up his communications with the future.   He belongs to that army
of the terrible meek who in spite of wars and dictators
may yet inherit the earth.

[19] *Culture and Anarchy,* p. 28.   Published by the Macmillan
Company.   Used by permission.

LOUIS PASTEUR

1822-1895

You may owe your life to Louis Pasteur. Thousands do. For he, more than any other scientist, gave us a knowledge of the nature of the action of germs in causing diseases in men and animals. He worked out methods whereby we can protect ourselves from certain diseases and minimize their poisons. He was the first to teach us to sterilize surgical instruments. Gangrene followed a large proportion of surgical operations as well as ordinary wounds. Prior to his discoveries infections following childbirth took a fearful toll of human life. Contagious diseases were apt to become pestilential in scope and fatal in intensity. The daily milk supply of multitudes in the cities carried germs of deadly maladies.

A Plodder. If you saw the motion picture "The Life of Louis Pasteur," you will recall Paul Muni's admirable portrayal of the great scientist in the midst of his battles against germs on the one hand and intrenched ignorance and prejudice on the other. That film concentrated its attention upon the achievements of the mature man. In this sketch we shall not omit these, but we shall concern ourselves more with his earlier struggles as a boy and young man. We shall observe the process by which he gradually shaped his purpose and formed those habits of work and character which made the foundation of his later accomplishments. Brilliant as is the record of those accomplishments, his biography is not the story of a genius or a prodigy. It is the story of a plodder who was always outdistanced in his school work by the bright boys of the class. It is the old story of the tortoise and the hare.

The chief source of our information is the monumental biography of Pasteur by René Vallery-Radot, translated from the French by Mrs. R. L. Devonshire with an introduction by Sir William Osler. No other account of his life is so thoroughly documented or so packed with human interest. And no other keeps a better balance in treatment of the man and the scientist. In his introduction Sir William Osler singles out three lessons which he says young men of science may learn from the life of Pasteur: first, the value of method or technique; second, the importance of one's friendships; and third, the virtue of "humility before the unsolved problems of the Universe." How Pasteur's story illustrates these, and how he developed the power to win his battles in science, we shall presently see.

Son of a Tanner. Born in the humble home of a tanner in Dôle, France, on December 27, 1822, there was nothing in his surroundings to give promise of an other-than-ordinary future. But the blood in his veins, could it have spoken, might have prophesied hope. On his father's side his ancestors had been tillers of the soil for four generations. Originally serfs, one of them—Claude Etienne Pasteur—purchased his freedom in 1763 and henceforth he and his son and grandson had been tanners by trade. None of them had much schooling, but they took pride in the quality of the leather they tanned.

In 1811 Joseph Pasteur—later to become Louis' father—was conscripted at the age of twenty in the army of Napoleon. For the next three years he fought in many a battle of the Peninsular War. In a regiment which gained the reputation of "brave amongst the brave" because it so frequently fought against far superior numbers, Joseph worked his way up from private to corporal to sergeant to sergeant-major and won the cross of the Legion of Honor. Like most of his comrades he became passionately devoted to Napoleon whose dazzling victories had stirred the imaginations of his men to visions of Empire and world conquest. Napoleon's fall and his own discharge from services were bitter gall to sergeant-major Joseph Pasteur. But he—a veteran at twenty-three—resigned himself to his lot and returned to the mundane business of tanning in the village of Besançon. He lived by himself, a lonely but peaceful man, until one day an order came that he, like other soldiers of Napoleon's former army, must surrender his sword to the city authorities. Joseph

Pasteur surrendered his sword. But when, a little later, he saw that it had been given to a local policeman —*his* sword, symbol to him of the glory of Napoleon —he was unable to restrain himself. He leaped upon the policeman, wrestled with him, and came off with the precious sword which no one thereafter tried to take from him.

Joseph Pasteur had a crude and undeveloped talent for painting. On an inner door of his house, some years after Louis was born, he painted a picture of a soldier in a bedraggled Napoleonic uniform. The soldier has turned peasant and leans upon his spade while he dreams of the victories of the past. But Joseph wasted little time in such recollections. Quiet, sober, industrious, and honest, he plied his trade and built up for himself a reputation of furnishing the best tanned leather that bootmakers could obtain anywhere. At twenty-five he married Jeanne Etiennette Roqui, daughter of a family of gardeners who lived just across the river from his tannery.

His Mother. This girl, who became the mother of Louis Pasteur, came from "one of the oldest plebeian families of the country," a family noted for its strong affections. "To love like the Roqui" meant to have a feeling for one's kin that was deep, loyal, and lasting. She was her husband's complement, active where he was slow, gay where he was grave, enthusiastic where he was cautious. Married in 1815, the young Pasteurs moved to Dôle, where they began to raise their own

131

family. Their first child died in infancy. Next came a daughter and four years later—in 1822—their first and only son, Louis. Two daughters were born in the years following.

In botanical laboratories these days we frequently have an ingenious camera arrangement by which motion pictures are taken at periodic intervals of the growth of some plant. Let us imagine we have such a camera and that we focus it upon various stages in the growth of Louis Pasteur.

Our first picture shows him a happy youngster of four years, playing in the tannery yard with other boys of the neighborhood. They have only bits of iron and bark for toys, but what imaginative boy needs more? Occasionally they fish in the river or trap in the adjacent woods. But Louis will take no part in the trapping. He cannot bear to see the pain of a wounded lark. But the camera, because it possesses no sense of smell, leaves out an important element in this scene. It does not give us the ever-present odor of the tannery yard. Years later when homesickness oppressed him he would say, "If I could only get a whiff of the tannery yard I feel I should be cured." [1]

Early Schools. Next we see him in the primary school of the town of Arbois to which his family has moved. He is the smallest scholar and perhaps to compensate for this handicap he strives to excel in his

[1] This and the following quotations in this sketch are from *The Life of Louis Pasteur,* by R. Vallery-Radot, reprinted with permission from Doubleday, Doran and Company, Inc.

studies so that he may be appointed monitor over less advanced pupils. Whether or not he succeeds in becoming a monitor we do not know. Probably not, for he is slow and cautious, and when he passes into a higher school his teacher rates him only as a "good average" student.

Our next picture shows him a lad of about twelve. He is seated at a homemade easel making a pastel drawing of his mother. She wears a white cap, a simple dress, and a blue and green tartan shawl. It is only a childish attempt, of course, but the lines are bold and Vallery-Radot says of it, "The portrait is full of sincerity and not unlike the work of a conscientious pre-Raphaelite." His boyish friends have dubbed him "the artist."

While we are watching Louis draw the portrait of his mother it may be well to consider for a moment three friends of the family who occasionally drop in to spend an evening. One is an old army doctor attached to the local hospital. He is a man who "studies for the sake of learning and who does a great deal of good while avoiding popularity." Another is the village philosopher and historian who has many a tale of the courage of the Arboisians of earlier generations. The third is the headmaster of the College of Arbois. He is one of those rare teachers who have a creative influence on their students, kindling their imaginations and stirring their ambitions. He has discovered a spark in young Louis and in the days to come he will fan it into flame. Others had seen the boy's slowness and had thought him only a faithful plodder. This teacher sees that his slowness comes from his desire to be absolutely sure of himself, and that back of it lies a curious and eager mind. He takes long walks with Louis, talking to him of his future and of the possibility of trying to enter the great Ecole Normale in Paris. This is the school that trains the young professors of France. Candidates for it must be under twenty-one years of age. They may enter only after they are already in possession of their bachelor's degree, have passed rigid entrance examinations, and have signed an agreement to devote ten years to public instruction under the Ministry of Education. Louis listens with sparkling eyes.

First Defeat. Four years pass. We see him now in Paris in the Barbet Boarding School whither he has come to work for his bachelor's degree. (In France it is a much more elementary degree than in England or America.) He is fourteen and has something of his father's reserve and his mother's passionate love of kinsfolk. The two traits are working to his disadvantage. For he is homesick. Probably never was a boy more acutely so. Were it not for his reserve he could ease his grief by pouring it out to his fellows. He tries to overcome it. He tells himself this is Paris, the magnificent city. This is his big opportunity to prepare for the Ecole Normale and a career as a professor. He and his family have been striving for just

134

this chance for him. It is of no use. Night after night he lies awake thinking of home. If he could only smell a whiff of that old tannery yard again! Finally, the headmaster, fearful for the boy's health, writes to his father. A few days later Louis is told that someone wants to see him in a nearby café. He goes and finds a familiar figure seated at a table, his head in his hands. The man looks up. "I have come to fetch you," he says. No need for explanations. Father and son understand each other's feeling.

A Long Struggle. Three years later. Louis at seventeen is now at the college of Besançon, which is only about fifty miles from his home. When his father had taken him back to Arbois the boy had abandoned his ambition to prepare for the Ecole Normale. He had returned to the local college of Arbois and to his easel. He had begun to draw and paint again. He drew the village folk, the notary, the cooper, an old nun, a little boy, the registrar of mortgages, the mayor, and the various members of the Roch family. These drawings are still preserved and are said to have considerable merit. In the school he had applied himself with such vigor that at the end of the year ne had "walked off with more prizes than he could carry." Again the kindly headmaster had talked to him of preparing for the Ecole Normale. Fearing only a repetition of his homesickness if he went again to the preparatory school in Paris, he had chosen Besançon where his father might visit him occasionally. It is a more advanced college than the one at Arbois and the philosophy master, himself a former student at the Ecole Normale and a graduate of the University of Paris, is keen in his understanding of Louis' mind. He perceives his slowness to be rooted in caution. Some day it will flower in the thoroughness of a scientific mind. He encourages Louis to keep steadily on in his studies. Our picture shows the boy standing before his three examiners at the end of the year and listening to their verdict—"good in Greek on Plutarch and Latin on Virgil, good also in rhetoric, composition, medicine, history, geography, and philosophy, very good in elementary science." And with that verdict they bestow upon him the degree of Bachelor of Letters.

"Good, good . . . very good," but these and his degree are not enough to admit him to the Ecole Normale. They are only the first hurdles. Competitive entrance examinations must be passed. The headmaster knows Louis is not yet ready for them. To help him as well as to ease his own administrative burdens he offers Louis the post of preparation master at the College of Besançon. It will give him the opportunity to take advanced work in mathematics while he acts as a mentor to his fellow students in the preparation of their lessons. A year or two at this and then he may be able to tackle the competitive examinations. Louis accepts. It is his first remunerative employment.

A year later we find him on a Sunday morning in church, reading a book during the service. The book is *An Essay on the Art of Being Happy,* by Joseph Droz. For Louis is taking seriously the business of developing his inner strength. He feels that had there not been some weakness in him he could have overcome the homesickness that had wrecked his first attempt at school in Paris. So he has deliberately set out to strengthen his moral fiber. Among the exercises he employs to this end he gives first place to the reading of good books, especially the works of Joseph Droz. In Droz's philosophy he catches glimpses of a "religion free from all controversy and all intolerance, a religion of peace, love, and devotion." That is the sort of religion he wants.

A sense of altruism begins to stir within him, for he writes again to suggest that he pay for the schooling of his younger sister Josephine in a girls' college. "I could easily do it by giving private lessons." But his parents refuse to accept this sacrifice. Instead they offer to supplement his small salary by an allowance that would permit him to take private lessons and so prepare himself more thoroughly for the competitive examinations. They compromise on the *status quo.*

No picture of Louis Pasteur's life at Besançon is complete without the figure of his student comrade Charles Chappuis. A lithograph which Louis made of him (a lithograph so well done that it won the author a place in a book entitled "Les Graveurs du XIXme Siècle") shows him a gentle-faced youth. The son of a wise and concientious notary, he had a sense of responsibility

137

beyond the average for boys of his age. He and Louis formed a David and Jonathan friendship which lasted throughout their lives. Their paths diverged in time, as Charles went in for a career in teaching philosophy and Louis for one in Science, but they never lost their affectionate interest in each other. In Besançon they shared their adolescent problems, dreams, disappointments, and hopes.

Family, friends, literature—each of these made a profound contribution to the life of Pasteur. Each had a place apart, a kind of private chapel in the temple of his heart.

Meanwhile the competitive examinations ever loomed upon the horizon. He saw fellow-students with a brilliance he did not possess come up for them and fail. He was doing well in physics, but mathematics proved a constant battle. After a long wrestle with this formidable foe he wrote, "One ends by having nothing but figures, formulas, and geometrical forms before one's eyes." Nevertheless it was the accuracy he was gaining from mathematics that became the outstanding characteristic of many of his later researches.

But to return to our pictures. We see him at nineteen sitting along with twenty-one other students at the College of Besançon taking a preliminary examination to see whether or not they are ready to try for the entrance tests at the Normale. Louis comes out fifteenth in this test. The authorities grant him permission to go on and take the competitives, but he decides against it. His standing is too low. He will take another year. He will go to Paris, back to the same school which had been the scene of his defeat by homesickness. He will go now not as a lonely boy from the country but as one who has strengthened his will and his inner resources and has had some experience in teaching.

So to the Barbet Boarding School he returns. He earns two-thirds of his expenses by teaching mathematics to younger pupils from six to seven in the morning. He is too busy to be homesick. In addition to his studies and his tutoring he attends lectures at the Sorbonne, where a celebrated chemist, J. B. Dumas, makes that subject so vivid and appealing that Louis is inspired with an enthusiasm for it. He calls himself a "disciple" of M. Dumas. For the first time his purpose begins to be specific. He will major in chemistry.

He Wins a Victory. One year of this strenuous preparation and the great day arrives for the competitives for entrance into the Normale. Louis feels he is ready now. In fact he must be ready now or never, for he is nearly twenty-one, the upper age limit for candidates. He takes the examination and the judges rank him fourth on the list of those admitted. He is so eager to enter that he arrives at the Normale several days before the opening of its school year. He is allowed to sleep in the empty dormitory. The following morning he calls upon M. Barbet to express his gratitude in a tangible form for all the kindness the master had shown him in the years of his preparation. He volunteers to come each Thursday morning at six o'clock and teach M. Barbet's boys physical science. Barbet accepts. "I am very pleased," writes Louis' father, learning of this, "that you are giving lessons at M. Barbet's. He has been so kind to us. . . . It will encourage him to show the same kindness to other studious young men, whose future might depend upon it." This is typical of his father's letters—encouraging, affectionate, but never sentimental. Back in Arbois the hopes and pride of the tanner and his family focus upon the young scholar in Paris.

And so Louis Pasteur won his first long battle for a higher education. It was far more than simply a conquest of elementary academic subjects. It was chiefly a long period of persevering discipline to strengthen his own will, to develop his own mental and spiritual habits. It marked the end of the epoch of the country boy from the tannery yard and the beginning of the young scientist. At the age of twenty-one he stands upon the threshold of an unknown career, but equipped with an integrity of character, an ability to study, a love of good literature, and the loyalty of family, friends, and teachers. He is a slow student but a thorough one, and he already has two of the lovely graces—gratitude and generosity.

He has won his first battle, but greater ones await him. He must make good at the Ecole. He has attained a place among the picked young minds of France. Many excel him in quickness and in brilliance. Just to stay with them is no small undertaking. His professors have large classes and are among the busiest men in Paris. What can he do to gain their attention? The science in which he proposes to major is still undeveloped. A hundred conflicting theories in chemistry put forth their claims to his allegiance. He must test them, discard the false and hold to the true. He must so make himself the master of some area of chemistry that he can secure his doctorate in it and be prepared to teach it in some college faculty. This is as far ahead as he can see just now. It may be well that the future veils from his view the struggles with the physicians and surgeons and theologians.

Begins Experimental Work. We see him next some months after his entrance at the Normale. He is in a laboratory conducting a simple experiment of his own. (Laboratories in those days, even in the best of schools, were crude, makeshift affairs in attics or cellars. School budgets did not provide for them, and professors had to equip them out of their own meager salaries.) Louis has listened to a lecture on the process of obtaining phosphorus. Most of the students have been content to take the professor's word for it. Louis asks permission to use the professor's laboratory to work out the process firsthand. He buys some bones, burns them, and treats the ash with sulphuric acid. He extracts some sixty grams of phosphorus, puts it in a bottle and labels it. Anyone who has thus worked out for himself some scientific problem knows the sense of victory and confidence that comes with the pasting of that label on the finished product. Louis becomes known as the student who works out things for himself.

Because he is slow and has to compete daily with quicker minds, he must emulate the tortoise in his race with the hare, plodding steadily on. Thus another picture of him about this time shows him spending a Sunday afternoon, as he spent most of his holidays, in a laboratory at the Sorbonne. He is working on a problem that has bothered chemists for years. It is the origin of an acid called paratartaric. His professors have been unable to solve the problem, partly because the paratartaric acid is very rare. If Louis can obtain a small quantity of it, he may be able to discover its origin by certain experiments on its crystals. The origin established might lead to an understanding of similar problems in crystallography.

Plodding On. Five years later Louis is still on this problem, not exclusively, of course, but persistently. He hears of possible small supplies of paratartaric acid in Germany, Austria, and Italy, and like a hound on a long scent he is off to those countries in search of the precious liquid. The story of that search, exciting though it is, is too long for this short sketch. In the end he returns empty-handed, having discovered that the scientists who thought they had it had something else instead. He is practically empty-pocketed as well, for he has spent his savings on the fruitless search. Back into his own laboratory he goes, and after months

142

of dogged labor, finally succeeds in making paratartaric acid directly from tartaric acid. He telegraphs the news to the professor who has guided him in his studies through these years.

It may sound purely acadamic to us today, but to the scientists of the middle of the last century it was well-nigh as startling as the discovery of radium.

This was one of his research projects. Others included *"Researches into the saturation capacity of arsenious acid,* a study of the arsenites, of potash, soda, and ammonia," *"Study of the phenomena relative to the rotary polarization of liquids," "Researches in dimorphism."* Each of these he wrote up in detail.

Small wonder that a student with such a passion for original research—for finding things out for himself—should attract the attention of his professors. Two of these professors had such a profound influence upon his life that snapshots of them belong among the pictures of Pasteur.

One is M. Balard, a young instructor, who had once been an apothecary's pupil, and at the age of twenty-four had gained fame as the discoverer of bromin. He took Louis into his own laboratory, and insisted upon letting him be allowed to stay and work there when the Minister of Public Instruction would have sent Louis, before he had obtained his doctorate, to teach physics in a small and remote college.

The other was Biot, a grand old scientist with a warm heart beneath a crusty exterior. Balard told him

about Pasteur's researches on paratartaric acid. Biot
was skeptical of the reputed result, for he had done
much work himself in this field, but when Pasteur
went to Biot's own laboratory and demonstrated his
method and findings, the old man took the young one by
the arm and said, "My dear boy, I have loved science
so much during my life that this touches my very
heart." Thereafter he counted himself Pasteur's spon-
sor and presented his later researches to the scientific
world that centered in Paris.

With such friends to encourage him and such disciplined ability to concentrate on his research projects
(he would occasionally become so concentrated that he
would shut himself in the laboratory for weeks at a
time), he forged steadily ahead. The tortoise was over-
taking the hares of his class at the Normale. At the
end of the second year fourteen of them went up for the
advanced competitive examinations by which professors
were recruited for the faculties and secondary schools
of France. Only four passed. Louis was third. He
was not satisfied with this and pressed on toward the
doctorate, not so much for the honor as for the pure
joy he found in the work.

Strong Home Ties. Meanwhile he kept fresh his
interest and affection for his home. His letters to his
parents and sisters report his projects in detail, and they
in turn keep him posted in regard to the tannery business and the doings in the home and village. When
Louis learns of a new tanning process, he describes it

144

to his father. When the father learns of some favor or encouragement given by a scientist to his son, he writes the man a simple but dignified and gracious note of thanks. When the parent deplores his own lack of knowledge of grammar and some of the mathematical principles with which Louis is wrestling, the son becomes his father's tutor (on the pretext that "you may be able to help Josephine," although Josephine's enthusiasm for knowledge seems to have been distinctly under control) and sends him a series of lessons by mail—lessons that often keep the elder Pasteur working far into the night. When the son in a burst of enthusiastic patriotism donates all his savings—about one hundred and fifty francs—to the "holy cause of the republic" during the exciting days of the Revolution of 1848, the father urges that he publish the fact in one of the leading national journals in this fashion, "Gift to the patrie: one hundred and fifty francs, by the son of an old soldier of the Empire, Louis Pasteur of the Ecole Normale." In this same letter he suggests that Louis "raise a subscription in your school in favor of the poor Polish exiles who have done so much for us. It would be a good deed." Although his father did most of the writing for the family, Louis' mother and sisters shared the same bonds of affection. "You are absolutely everything to them," his father wrote. One day in the midst of his work Louis received word that his mother was stricken with a fatal illness. He hastened to her side, but she passed away before he arrived.

His grief was so intense that for weeks he could do nothing in his beloved laboratory.

Begins Teaching. When he did return, he plunged again into his researches with such vigor that he soon completed the work for his doctorate. He would gladly have stayed on in Paris pursuing these researches further under the tutelage of Biot whose favorite protégé he had become, but when he had entered the Normale, he had signed the engagement required of all its students—namely, that he would give ten years to teaching under the Ministry of Public Instruction—and now the time comes when the Ministry calls for the fulfillment of this bond. He is assigned to the Dijon Lycée as professor of physics. It is not a very desirable position, and Biot protests heartily, but to no avail. To Dijon he goes in November, 1848, at the age of twenty-five.

And here let us resume our scenes. The next has an atmosphere almost gloomy. It shows Pasteur in the small secondary school trying to master the art of teaching elementary science to first- and second-year youngsters whose chief characteristic often seems a capacity to resist the acquisition of knowledge. The classes are large—eighty in one of them. The boys know nothing and care less about the original researches their new professor has been making under the masters in Paris. The ambition of most of them seems to be to get passing grades with as little inconvenience as possible. Their thoughts are on their games and their personal affairs. Even the few ambitious ones have their ambitions centered around themselves, not science and certainly not their professor. So it has always been with teen-age pupils and so it will probably continue to be time without end. The teacher's job is to lift them out of themselves, to kindle their interest in learning, to make them want to master the subject so that they may apply it to the service of humanity. Pasteur finds it no easy job. He lays aside his researches and devotes himself entirely to the art of teaching. "I find that preparing my lessons takes up a great deal of time," he writes Chappuis. "It is only when I have prepared a lesson very carefully that I succeed in making it very clear and capable of compelling attention. If I neglect it at all I lecture badly and become unintelligible." He finds great difficulty in holding the interest of the large class toward the end of the hour. To overcome this he introduces the practice of conducting experiments in their presence. This goes better, but even so, at the end of the year he is filled with discouragement. If he remains there he will have no more opportunity for research. The years will succeed themselves, and all his time and energy will be spent in trying to interest large classes of young boys in the elements of science.

The next scene is as full of joy as the last was of frustration. Less than two years have passed, but we find Pasteur now at the University of Strasburg as assistant professor of chemistry. His old professor friends at Paris have been unwilling to see him waste his years teaching elementary science in a secondary school.

147

They have kept after the Minister of Education and seen to it that the first available position in chemistry in an advanced school has been offered to Pasteur. Here he has older students, smaller classes, and an opportunity to carry on at least some of his own researches. Here, too, he can room with an old school friend, Bertin.

Courtship and Marriage. More important than any of these is the fact that he has met and fallen in love with Marie Laurent, daughter of the Rector of the Academy at Strasburg. In the Laurent home he has found the same ideals, the same spiritual values, the same affectionate and self-sacrificing good will that had given dignity and beauty to his own home at Arbois. Marie is a joyous girl who knows what is expected of a professor's wife. Eventually his proposal is accepted, and the marriage takes place on May 29, 1849. He finds in Marie every quality he could wish for in a wife. Among other virtues, as he sees it, she is quite willing to allow his work in the laboratory to come before everything else and to help him there in emergencies.

Growing Recognition. He is launched upon his career and is happy in it. He wants nothing better than to remain in Strasburg, develop his ability as a teacher, pursue his researches, and raise his family. His plan is simple enough. He will devote his vacation periods to his researches and present them each year to the Academy of Sciences. For a few years this plan works very well. The Academy receives his annual reports with increasing appreciation. Old Biot says of him, "He throws light on everything he touches." The Academy gives one whole sitting, January 3, 1853, to a review of his studies, especially those on paratartaric acid. As a result he receives the red ribbon of the Legion of Honor. (Imagine the joy of his father on Louis' next visit to Arbois when the two could take their Sunday afternoon walk together, each wearing the ribbon; the father's won on the field of battle under the great Napoleon, the son's in the laboratory under a more imperious master, Science.) The Pharmaceutical Society awards him a prize of fifteen hundred francs, half of which he spends in buying scientific instruments which the school is too poor to afford.

Triumphant though these years are for him, they are not without their disappointments. His researches are by no means invariably successful. Many of them lead him into blind alleys. A score of times after days of experiment he writes across the record "erroneous." Occasionally old Biot intervenes and dissuades him from a project on which he has started with great enthusiasm. Louis reluctantly accepts the advice of his aged friend and discontinues such a study. After abandoning the false leads he undertakes a study of the phenomenon of fermentation, not suspecting that he is starting on a project which in a few years will revolutionize the whole science of chemistry and have an incalculable influence on medicine as well. But that story must wait while we relate other events that change

the outer circumstances of his life, if not its inner
character and direction.

Five years after his appointment to Strasburg, the
Minister of Education asks him to become professor
and dean of the new faculty at Lille. It is a new
school and holds out the opportunity of new methods
of teaching as well as new equipment. It might become
the pathfinder for the future of science. Pasteur
accepts and on the day of the opening of the school
announces a great innovation: this school is to have a
laboratory for students where, for a small annual sum,
they may work out for themselves the principal experiments carried out before them in the classes. He thus
makes available for his new students the practical
method of learning that had distinguished his own un-
dergraduate work.

This sounds so commonplace to us today that it is
difficult to realize how radical a departure it was in
1854. Not a college in France had a laboratory where
students were expected to experiment for themselves.
As for Science itself, the man on the street saw little
connection between his daily problems and academic researches of the scientist. Pasteur's work from now on
is to change all this. He not only introduces laboratories for students, but takes the students on tours to
factories and foundries in northern France and Belgium
so that they may see for themselves the way work is
being done and return to their laboratories to improve
on the methods if they can. By such innovations he

soon builds up for the new school a reputation as the most progressive educational institution in France.

Experiments in Ferments. One day shortly after the opening of the school a local manufacturer with a problem on his mind comes into the office of the young dean. The manufacturer's business is making alcohol from beetroot. Of late he has been having poor success with his product. The fermentation process seems sickly. Will Pasteur help by finding out where the trouble lies? He will. He spends several days at the factory and returns to his laboratory with various samples of the ferment. He examines these, noting the difference between the healthy and sickly liquids. Until now scientists have rejected the idea that fermentation is caused directly by any active form of life. They have held that "it was the dead portion of the yeast, that which had lived and was being altered, which acted upon sugar." For three years (frequently interrupted by administrative and other duties) he conducts his experiments. They involve also the fermentation of milk. Finally, in 1857, he announces his discovery that the *ferment is itself an active microorganism.* He has isolated it and now presents his findings to the Lille Scientific Society and later to the Academy of Sciences. The manufacturer has waited a long time for his answer, but when it comes it gives not only the answer to his own problem, providing him and all others in the alcohol business with the way to secure healthy ferments, but furnishes the key to the solution of a multitude of other problems infinitely greater than the manufacture of alcohol as we shall soon see. The presence of microorganisms as the cause of fermentation suggests to Pasteur's eager mind the possibility that similar organisms may also be the cause of a similar phenomenon—namely, putrefaction in diseases. If that should turn out to be true . . .

But before this idea shapes itself definitely in his mind or he has an opportunity to institute further researches, another change in his outer circumstances takes place. He is asked to become the administrative head of the Ecole Normale. How he could consider leaving the new school at Lille after only a few years there would be inexplicable to anyone who did not know the affection he had for his Alma Mater. In the vicissitudes of politics and educational change, it had fallen on evil days. It needed new blood, new imagination, new methods. Pasteur had them, and he felt that he owed them to the school which had nurtured them. His new duties would require not only a general administration of the school and the direction of its scientific studies, but also "the surveillance of the economic and hygienic management, the care of general discipline, intercourse with the families of the pupils, and the literary or scientific establishments frequented by them." Old Biot strenuously objects because he sees that the Normale will not give Pasteur adequate laboratories for his researches and that the administrative duties will rob him of time which ought to be spent in experimentation. For once Pasteur does not follow the advice of his old friend. This, he feels, is not a matter of science but one of his own personal loyalty to an old school which needs him.

Headmaster of the Normale. He accepts the call and takes up his duties under the most discouraging circumstances. The old buildings are dark and gloomy, the faculty run down, there is only one laboratory and that the private domain of the professor of physics. Pasteur has no assistant of any kind. But he has a stout heart and he knows what he wants. He brings new men to the faculty. He converts a garret into a new laboratory. He introduces the progressive methods of teaching he has used at Lille. He modernizes the old buildings as far as a limited budget will permit. He inaugurates an annual journal called *Scientific Annals of the Ecole Normale* as a means of keeping the alumni of the school in touch with its new researches. Gradually the spirit of the student body undergoes a transformation. The students take a new interest in their work and some of them (probably not all, as Vallery-Radot in his enthusiasm seems to imply) develop a passion for study. They are difficult years for Pasteur, but he at least has the reward of seeing his beloved old school rehabiliated in the eyes of the country as well as in its own self-esteem. And somehow he manages in that garret laboratory a series of researches that result in providing a new basis for the study of diseases in animals and in human beings.

153

A Famous Controversy. With one of these researches we shall now deal. From the times of Ancient Greece poets, philosophers, theologians, and most naturalists had accepted the theory that minute forms of life had come into existence spontaneously—that is, without parents of their own kind. It is called the theory of Spontaneous Generation. Even up to the seventeenth century no one had seriously questioned it. One naturalist in the sixteenth century had held that all one needed to create mice was a receptacle of dirty linen and a bit of cheese. An Italian named Buoanni had taught that a "certain timberwood after rotting in the sea produced worms which engendered butterflies, and these butterflies became birds." This spontaneous generation theory had fallen into disrepute until the invention of the miscroscope gave it new birth. Those myriads of miscroscopic forms that one could see through the powerful lenses, surely they didn't go through the reproductive processes of plants and animals? One day —December 20, 1858—a well-known and reputable scientist, M. Pouchet, presented to the Academy of Sciences a report entitled, "A Note on Vegetable and Animal Proto-organisms Spontaneously Generated in Artificial Air and in Oxygen Gas." He claimed to have demonstrated the truth of the old theory.

Germs in Air. Some days later we find Pasteur in his garret laboratory reading a copy of that paper and underlining certain statements which he intends to subject to strict experimentation. The fundamental question, he determines, is whether or not the air in such experiments as Pouchet has prosecuted was only air— that is, a pure mixture of the component gases—or did it contain germs? He will conduct his own experiments to test for the presence of germs in air. He begins by drawing air through a small tube in which he has inserted a filter. The filter becomes covered with dust, and this dust upon examination he finds to contain germs and spores. After a year of such careful observations made under varying circumstances, Pasteur concludes that there is nothing in air itself that will produce life other than the germs which it carries.

But a M. Joly and his pupil, Charles Musset, join Pouchet, and thus backed, Pouchet multiplies his arguments in favor of spontaneous generation and his objections to Pasteur's conclusions. Pasteur keeps quiet and continues with his work. He invents little flasks with long, narrow, hooked necks. These he fills with an easily alterable liquid and awaits results. The air can get to the liquid through the neck, but the germs are deposited on the curve of the tube before they can come in contact with the contents of the flask. Only when the flasks are tipped so that the germs and the alterable liquid come together does alteration occur.

Pouchet wants to know "how could germs contained in the air be numerous enough to develop in every organic infusion? Such a crowd of them would produce a thick mist as dense as iron." To Pasteur this is the hardest question to answer. Can it be that the germ

155

content of the air varies according to locale? He takes a large number of flasks, fills them with an easily corruptible fluid, boils them free of germs, draws the necks of the flasks to vertical points, and while they are still boiling, seals them so that all air is shut out. Then he sets out with his flasks to open them in divers places and await results. One set he takes high up a mountain side in the Alps where the air is almost if not quite free of dusts. Another set he takes into a courtyard in Paris where the air is heavy and fetid. With infinite precaution he gathers the air. He finds that only one of the twenty flasks opened in the high altitude shows any alteration in the liquid whereas all the flasks opened in the courtyard show alteration. From this and many similar experiments he concludes: "That it can be affirmed that the dusts suspended in atmospheric air are the exclusive origin, the necessary condition of life in infusions."

The advocates of spontaneous generation are not quieted, however. They still insist that air alone is necessary for the creation of germs. They make experiments similar to his own in the effort to refute him by his own methods. The flasks they open in high altitudes show alteration. Therefore, they conclude, Pasteur is wrong and we are right. But Pasteur insists that they have not known how to experiment and must not have taken proper precautions.

Spontaneous Generation Refuted. The spontaneous generation leaders request the Academy of Sciences to decide the matter. A commission is appointed. The commission asks both sides to present experiments in its presence. Twice it fixes dates for the demonstrations. On both occasions the spontaneous generation advocates decline to make their experiments under the conditions set. Thereupon the Academy decides in favor of Pasteur, who not only demonstrated before them but before a huge popular audience at the Sorbonne in the presence of the leading scientific, literary, and philosophical lights of the day. "M. Pasteur's experiments are decisive," pronounced the head of the Academy. "If spontaneous generation is real, what is required to obtain animalculae? Air and putrescible liquor. M. Pasteur puts air and putrescible liquor together and nothing happens. Therefore spontaneous generation is not."

This settles the matter for most of the scientists, but not for many a philosopher, journalist, and theologian. The echoes of their arguments reverberate through the magazines and forums of the next decade, but eventually die away.

Purpose. One sentence in Pasteur's report contains the germ of his future work: "What would be most desirable would be to push those studies far enough to prepare the road for a serious research into the origin of various diseases." Pushing those studies on gradually becomes the consuming purpose of his life. They include the study of the silkworm disease, of septicemia, of childbed fever, of chicken cholera (and an amazing extension of Jenner's discovery of the principle of vaccines), of anthrax and of hydrophobia. All of these stem from Pasteur's investigation into the cause of fermentation and the discovery that it was due to an active microorganism. The results of these studies have made Pasteur's name a household word in every civilized country. They have saved countless thousands of lives. But not one of them came easily. In every case, in spite of his mounting series of successes, he had to meet and overcome the opposition of scientists as well as of officials and laymen. And he had to carry on in the face of national disaster and of personal griefs, illness and disappointments that would have brought despair to a less disciplined spirit. We shall view these projects briefly, noting how they lead step by step to an understanding of the way diseases are spread and the methods by which they can be prevented or their poisons minimized.

First, *the silkworm studies.* The cultivation of silkworms provided the daily bread of tens of thousands of people in southern France. In recent years a strange disease—pébrine—had afflicted the worms and spread to epidemic proportions. At first the cultivators had been able to procure seed (eggs from which silkworms were hatched) from other countries—Italy, Spain, Austria, China, Japan—but soon these countries too were invaded by the disease. The industry came to a standstill and the people dependent upon it to extreme poverty. J. B. Dumas, the chemist and now a Senator from one of the silkworm districts, appealed to his former pupil, Pasteur, to study the causes of the disease, saying that the distress among his constituents was unimaginable. Pasteur hesitated only for a moment. He was eager to do anything that might relieve that distress, but he knew nothing about silkworms, had never even touched one. Nevertheless he had confidence in his ability to study and to make experiments, and he had already won one battle with microorganisms of disease. He secured a temporary release from the Ecole Normale, read all he could find on the history of silkworms, journeyed to southern France, and took up his headquarters at Alais in the midst of the stricken region. It was a scene of desolation. "A traveler coming back to the Cévennes Mountains after an absence of fifteen years," he wrote, "would be saddened to see the change wrought in that countryside within such a short time. . . . The mulberry plantations are abandoned, . . . faces once beaming with health and good humor are now sad and drawn." The cultivators who still held on were trying desperately a hundred different cures, some suggested by pseudo-scientists, some by unscrupulous seed salesmen, and some by superstition. Let us watch Pasteur set about his task.

He begins by doubting all these alleged cures. He questions nurserymen, collects eggs, moths, and worms in various stages of the disease, sets up his microscope, and observes. After months of study (interrupted and saddened by the death of his father and of two of his daughters) he comes to the conclusion that the "evil de-

159

velops chiefly in the chrysalis at the moment of the moth's formation, on the eve of the function of reproduction. The microscope then detects its presence with certitude, even when the seed and the worm seem very healthy." He states his hypothesis thus: "Every moth containing corpuscles must give birth to diseased seed." (The name "corpuscle" had been given to the little, black, pepper-like spots which appeared on diseased moths and worms.) The next problem, therefore, is to find some infallible method of procuring healthy seed. Such seed can only come from healthy moths. Every moth he examines is already infected. At last he finds two or three apparently healthy couples and receives as a gift four others from a neighboring town. With this small colony he begins the production of new seed, watching every stage in its development to see that no corruption might enter. It is a slow process. The silkworm producers become impatient and demand immediate results. They attack Pasteur for wasting time and the government because it has sent them a "mere chemist" instead of a competent zoologist or silkworm cultivator. "Have patience," urges Pasteur; but men on the brink of ruin have little patience. Yet Pasteur cannot hurry the reproductive and molting processes of his little colony. He must wait until the following spring for results.

The experiments at first turn out exactly as he predicts. He develops sixteen broods of worms and all seem healthly. Then, just as success seems assured, comes a serious setback. The sixteenth brood perishes almost immediately after the first molting. Their bodies rot rapidly, and yet there are no signs of corpuscles. Now it is for Pasteur to apply to himself the admonition he had given the cultivators—have patience. Easier to preach than to practice. But he brings his microscope into action, consults the work of former students of silkworms, and finally is convinced that these worms have not died of the same disease that had wrought the previous havoc, but of a different one known as flacherie.

Once more he returns to his experiments, this time to find how to conquer this second disease. He must raise new broods of worms from seed and check the whole cycle of reproduction step by step. It will take further months. The impatience of the cultivators mounts again and the seed salesmen multiply their efforts to discredit Pasteur. His father-in-law writes to his wife, "It is being reported here that the failure of Pasteur's process has excited the population of your neighborhood so much that he has had to flee from Alais, pursued by infuriated inhabitants throwing stones at him." The opposition was not as violent as that, but it was bad enough.

Surprises the Emperor. While waiting for the new broods to hatch and for his assistants to check the various stages of their progress during the following months, Pasteur busies himself with other projects. **He studies cholera,** dangerously but unsuccessfully.

"Studies of this sort," observes a fellow scientist, "require much courage." "What about duty?" answers Pasteur. He goes to the Palace of Campeigne, along with a company of other first-rank scientists of the country, as a guest of the Emperor. There the Emperor singles him out and asks him to tell of his work with microorganisms. He has Pasteur send for his microscope and demonstrate before the court some of his experiments. The Emperor expresses surprise that he has not turned some of the discoveries to private profit. Pasteur replies simply, "In France scientists would consider that they lowered themselves by doing so." But shortly afterward he follows up the Emperor's interest with an impassioned plea for a new laboratory for the Ecole Normale. The Emperor approves, obtains from his cabinet an appropriation, and the actual work of excavating for the new building is begun.

Paralysis. And now, just as he is plunging again into his silkworm studies, he is stricken with paralysis. For days he lies at the point of death. The modest home in Paris, adjoining the Ecole Normale, becomes the focus of anxious inquiries of the country's leading scientists who take turns watching at his bedside and tiptoeing to the study to convey news of his condition to their colleagues waiting there. They try to distract his thoughts from his work. He does not want them distracted. He believes that his end is near and he must make the most of his remaining hours. Utterly prostrate in body but clear in mind he insists on dictating a report on the "process for discovering in the earlier tests those (silkworm) eggs which are predisposed to flacherie." Slowly the paralysis retreats until only his left side is affected. He is allowed to sit up, then helped to a chair where he can look out of the window. What he sees from that window goads his desire to recover: the work on the new laboratory has been halted. The reason is evident: If he does not recover, the money will be used in some other way. Again Pasteur appeals to the Emperor, and the Emperor comes to his aid. Work on the laboratory is resumed.

A few weeks later he is back at his headquarters at Alais, accompanied by his wife and daughter to guard his frail health. He proceeds to establish the necessary methods to protect moths from both diseases and to select healthy seed. He reports these to the government. The government commission, to test their validity, asks him for a batch of healthy seed. Not only does he comply, but he sends additional samples and states positively what will occur in each instance. Lot No. 1 (of healthy seed) will succeed; lot No. 2 is of seed that will die exclusively of pébrine; lot No. 3 is of seed that will die exclusively of flacherie; and lot No. 4 is of seed that will die partly of pébrine and partly of flacherie. The commission is delighted at this unexpected compliance, and, when each of the lots turns out exactly as Pasteur had announced, they are convinced of the verity of his solution.

Routing the Quacks. But will these results be accepted? No. Pseudo-scientists have kept at their short-sighted insistence upon their own methods, and the seed merchants have continued to push the sale of their unhealthy seed with no regard for the benefit of the industry as a whole or of France. "You have quacks to fight and envy to conquer, probably a hopeless task," writes Dumas. "The best course is to march right through them, Truth leading the way. It is not likely that they will be converted or reduced to silence." Pasteur with the aid of his family and his assistants marches on. He piles up new proofs and verifications. He patiently instructs open-minded cultivators in his methods. Those who conscientiously follow out his instructions are rewarded with good seed, others with poor. Finally he is given a farm which has produced worms in the profitable days of the industry but has been devastated by the corpuscle and flacherie diseases. He carries out his methods here on a large scale and gives to the tenants twenty-five grams of good seed and keeps twenty-five for himself. His cause is almost ruined by an unscrupulous steward who sells some diseased Japanese seed along with that Pasteur has given him; but this is shortly cleared up, the farm makes its first profit in ten years, and Pasteur successfully completes a hard-fought conquest. "Nothing can repay you for your work," says the Mayor of Alais, "but the town of Alais will raise a golden statue to you." The golden statue did not materialize, but Pasteur had a greater reward: the gratitude of a people whose livelihood he had restored.

War Intervenes. Pasteur's plans for future investigations are brought to a painful halt by the Franco-Prussian War. Laboratories are converted to war uses, and the students of the Ecole Normale volunteer unanimously for military service. Pasteur, himself an ardent patriot, tries to enlist, but the lameness in his left leg and arm resulting from his paralytic stroke disqualifies him.

He returns to Arbois in a state of mental agony. Like many an idealist, he has believed that the advance of Science has been so international and has so convinced intelligent people that their real foes are in nature and not in each other, that war between two civilized nations is impossible. But now he must watch his students, including his own son, march away. He must observe scientists turning their energies to inventions of war. He must listen daily to the town crier announcing the casuality list and the grim advance of the Prussians toward Paris.

As Pasteur sees the desolation in the wake of the advance and hears of his neighbors in Arbois killed, his anguish increases. He must let the scientists of Germany know how one scientist of France looks upon this carnage. He writes to the University of Bonn, Germany, requesting it to take back the honorary doctor's degree it had bestowed upon him. A futile gesture, perhaps, but one could hardly expect the son of a soldier of Napoleon to remain placid under such stress. Still onward rolls the German military machine. Paris is besieged and bombarded, one bomb striking the Ecole Normale. Finally the city surrenders and the war is ended by a treaty ceding Alsace and Lorraine to Germany. Pasteur and his wife and daughter start out to find their son from whom they have not heard in months. An anxious business, but after days and nights of search they find him on a cart along the road from Paris. He has been ill and the reunited family devotes its immediate efforts to nursing him back to health.

Fighting Gangrene—and Surgeons. One of the appalling features of the war is the gangrene which has infected nearly every wound and followed nearly every surgical operation. Even in hospitals the mortality following amputation was over sixty per cent. An ambulance ward was the scene of "perpetual agony, the wounds of all the patients were suppurating, a horrible fetor pervaded the place, and infectious septicemia was everywhere." French doctors have been able to do nothing about it. Over in England, however, a great surgeon, Joseph Lister, who called himself a follower of Pasteur, had begun, in 1867, a new method of treating wounds. He sterilized his surgical instruments by passing them through a flame, and he took certain other elementary antiseptic precautions such as spraying the air with carbolic acid vapor and seeing to it that sponges and bandages were clean. Lister pursued these methods steadily until his hospital became noted for its large proportion of recoveries. One day Pasteur received a letter from Lister which gave the "mere chemist" a fresh impetus to apply his germ theory to infections of the human body.

My dear Sir . . . allow me to beg your acceptance of a pamphlet, which I send by the same post, containing an account of some investigations into the subject which you have done so much to elucidate, the germ theory of fermentative changes. I flatter myself that you may read with some interest what I have written on the organism which you were the first to describe. . . .
Allow me to take this opportunity to tender you my most cordial thanks for having, by your brilliant researches, demonstrated to me the truth of the germ theory of putrefaction, and thus furnished me with the principle upon which alone the antiseptic system can be carried out.

Fortified and encouraged by this communication from the great surgeon, Pasteur now begins to advise the surgeons at the Academy of Medicine to sterilize their instruments before using them. They understand so little the method of sterilization or the reasons for it that he must explain:

I mean that surgical instruments should merely be put through a flame, not really heated, and for this reason: if a wound were examined with a microscope, it would be seen that its surface presents grooves where dusts are harbored, which cannot be completely removed even by the most careful cleansing. Fire entirely destroys these organic dusts; in my laboratory, where I am surrounded by dust of all kinds, I never make use of an instrument without previously putting it through a flame.

The more alert surgeons accept the suggestion, and the proportion of their operations followed by gangrene begins to decline.

Meanwhile Pasteur pursues a series of experiments proving conclusively that gangrene, or septicemia, is caused by a microbe, which he isolates. He proves that the doctors and surgeons themselves have spread this germ by carrying it around on their instruments, their hands, and their clothing. But proving a thing and getting it accepted are different matters. Again he faces a host of detractors and unbelievers. The famous surgeon, Leon Le Fort, declares that Pasteur's theory "in its application to clinical surgery is absolutely inacceptable." Le Fort is supported by scores of others. But Pasteur persists and defends his findings by demonstrations before the Academy. He makes clear not only the cause of the disease but the necessity for *antiseptic* substances to kill or arrest the microbes and *aseptic* instruments, hands, and gauzes to safeguard the patient against receiving the microbes from doctors, surgeons, and nurses. In his defense he shows how this theory has grown naturally and inevitably from his previous work in fermentations and the silkworm disease. Gradually the opposition dies down and, in 1878, Pasteur has the satisfaction of hearing Dr. Sedillot read to the Academy a paper entitled "On the Influence of M. Pasteur's Work on Medicine and Surgery." The concluding sentence of that paper must have been balm to the spirit of the "mere chemist": "We shall have seen the conception and birth of a new surgery, a daughter of Science and Art, which shall be one of the great wonders of our century, and with which the names of Pasteur and Lister will remain gloriously connected."

Childbed Fever. It is a short step from the prevention of infection in wounds to Pasteur's next study—childbed fever. In 1864, 310 patients out of a total of 1,350 confinement cases in the Maternity Hospital of Paris had died of this disease. While this was extreme it was not unusual for one childbirth in five or six to be followed by the fever, often fatally. Pasteur sets himself to this problem with the same patient experimentation which had marked his earlier researches. One day he hears the doctors at the Academy discussing the disease, which is epidemic. They air various theories as to its cause. Pasteur interrupts. "None of those things causes the epidemic," he declares. "It is the nursing and medical staff who carry the microbe from an infected woman to a healthy one." This bombshell produces a violent effect and he is immediately challenged to prove that a microbe of this disease exists. Thereupon he goes to a blackboard and draws a picture of it, for he has isolated it in his laboratory. The doctors and nurses hardly relish the idea that they have been carriers of destruction, but Pas-

169

teur's demonstrations in the months that follow leave no room for doubt.

Without Salary. Much of this work on septicemia and childbed fever has been done without any monetary reward. Nor has he had a salary since ill-health had forced him to resign his professorship at the Sorbonne. (Still earlier he had resigned from the Ecole Normale.) He has declined a high salary in an agricultural school in Italy because he felt he was needed in France. France now expresses her appreciation. On the recommendation of the Academy the government bestows upon him a life annuity of 12,000 francs—a sum approximately equal to the salary he had had at the Sorbonne. With the bestowal comes the suggestion that he rest upon his laurels and enjoy life.

But how can he rest when millions of microbes are still unconquered and he knows more than anyone else their habits and deviltries? Let the ignorant rest, and the self-satisfied. He has work to do. That work is to free humanity from the terror of virulent diseases. "All my ambition," he declares, "is to arrive at the knowledge of putrid and contagious diseases."

Anthrax. One such disease—anthrax—is raging in eight of the agricultural provinces of France. From ten to fifty per cent of the sheep are affected and also many horses, cows, and oxen. Of late it has attacked human beings and 528 have died from it. Veterinarians and physicians have ascribed a score of causes for it, the chief being that it is due to some inanimate substance in

170

the soil. Acting on this theory, the veterinarians have advised that the sheep be removed to other regions supposedly unaffected. But soon the new regions are also found to be affected. A sheep would lag behind the flock, its head drooping and its breath labored. Its evacuations became bloody and in a few hours it would die. From any small rent in the skin would issue thick, black blood. (Hence the name "anthrax"—black blood. It was also called "splenic fever" or "charbon" because the spleen was found to be greatly distended and filled with a black liquid pulp.)

Pasteur begins his study of this disease by the same methods he has employed in his previous investigations, by reading what other scientists have written about it, by doubting prevalent theories, by observing every action of the sheep from health to death, and by examining under the microscope the food, the drink, the blood, the organs, the excreta, and the secretions of the body. He finds that two scientists in earlier years have already taken some of these steps. One, Devaine, in 1863, had declared that the cause of the disease was the presence in the blood of minute black rods which he called *bacteridia*. Another, a German physician named Koch, in 1876, had isolated these little rods and had succeeded in growing them in a culture outside the body. But no one had paid much attention to these discoveries and no one had yet followed them up with a cure. Pasteur's researches confirm the findings of these predecessors and go much further. He discovers how the disease is spread—by the spores of its microbes deposited on the grass or brought up in the intestines of earthworms from the graves of sheep dead of the disease. Next he discovers that the principle of vaccination (first used by Jenner in the treatment of smallpox) can be applied to healthy sheep. He has discovered this fact almost by accident while investigating chicken cholera. After a multitude of experiments he finds that he can vaccinate a sheep with a weakened solution of the virus of anthrax and that the animal so vaccinated will have only a mild attack of the disease.

Here is a point at which he can be challenged by his opponents. Chief of them is a man named Colin, a professor with a genius for negation. Behind him ranges a considerable company of men, mainly veterinarians, whose methods have thus far proved futile in checking the disease. One wonders why such men were not a bit wary about crossing swords with one who had had such signal successes in previous researches. But ignorance is seldom wary; that's why it is ignorance. And the numbers of these men give them courage. If Pasteur's fantastic notion about vaccinating sheep is valid, let him prove it among the flocks in the fields in sight of everyone, not simply in a Paris laboratory. Pasteur accepts the challenge. A provincial agricultural society offers him fifty healthy sheep for demonstration purposes. Conditions of the tests are agreed upon. Twenty-five of the sheep are to be vaccinated by two inoculations at twelve or fifteen days interval with some attenuated virus of anthrax. Some days later these twenty-five and the remaining twenty-five are to be inoculated with some virulent culture of anthrax. Pasteur is positive of the result. "The twenty-five unvaccinated sheep will all perish," he predicts, "the twenty-five vaccinated ones will survive."

News of the approaching test spreads throughout France. Newspapers focus the attention of the public upon the little farm near Melun where the drama will be enacted in May and June, 1882. The *Veterinary Press* warns that these experiments are crucial and that Pasteur's failure will mean the death of his reputation.

The vaccination of the first twenty-five sheep is duly made on May 5 and again on May 17. On May 31 these twenty-five and the remaining twenty-five unvaccinated sheep are given an inoculation of the concentrated virus. A day or two before that date Professor Colin warns of possible trickery on Pasteur's part. The latter's agents, Colin insinuates, may inoculate the vaccinated sheep with the top or weaker portion of the virus culture and the unvaccinated sheep with the bottom or heavy portion where the microbes will be most numerous. He advises his assistant to seize the bottle and shake it violently to secure a perfect mixture. Pasteur readily accepts this and other safeguards proposed by the suspicious. The inoculation takes place under conditions of perfect parity. Both sides await the results on June 5.

On the night of June 4 Pasteur cannot sleep. Of his theory he has no doubt, but he is experienced enough to know how many are the possible chances for errors in execution to creep in. On the morning of that day his agents have reported that two or three of the vaccinated sheep have temperatures and look a bit sickly. If he fails . . .

June 5 finally dawns and he makes his anxious way to the little farm where hundreds of veterinarians, doctors, farmers, and reporters have already gathered to see with their own eyes the results. There in the pen of the unvaccinated sheep lie twenty-two dead and three dying animals. In the other pen the twenty-five vaccinated sheep are in perfect health! The experiment is complete, the result decisive. Even the most incredulous are silenced—for the moment. Pasteur is awarded the grand cross of the Legion of Honor, and his two assistants, at his request, receive the cross of the Legion. But more important and gratifying by far is the fact that during the following year, 613,740 sheep and 83,946 oxen are vaccinated. Less than one per cent of the sheep and cattle die. The microbe army of anthrax is in full retreat.

Hydrophobia. Pasteur is now "at the boiling point," as he puts it. Each new conquest has given him an increased confidence for the next battle. Omitting several minor ones, we see him, in 1884, at the age of sixty-two, beginning a five-year study of hydrophobia, in many respects the most difficult as well as the most important of his career. The disease had become one of the major scourges of those days, striking frequently with terrible fatality. Men, women, and children as well as dogs were its victims. Although his aim primarily is to prevent hydrophobia in humans, Pasteur must make his experiments with animals, partly because he is unwilling to risk a human life and partly because—as his opponents never fail to remind him—he is a chemist and not a physician and, therefore, has no legal right to practice medicine in any form.

Following the same methods used in his former researches, his concentration is soon complete. His wife writes to their children, "Your father is absorbed in his thoughts, talks little, sleeps little, rises at dawn, and, in one word, continues the life I began with him this day thirty-five years ago." After about a year of the most arduous labor, much of it dangerous because he was dealing with rabid dogs whose bite would have been fatal to him, he is able to announce that the rabic virus invades the nervous centers, particularly the medulla oblongata, that he has produced a culture of the virus within living animals, that he can now obtain cultures of varying and controlled degrees of virulence, and finally, that he has obtained a preventive vaccine which has proved effective in making scores of dogs immune to the disease.

A Dramatic Test. As this news spreads, the question naturally arises, "He can make dogs immune—why not humans?" Pasteur replies, "When I shall have multiplied examples of the prophylaxis of rabies in dogs, I think my hand will tremble when I go on to mankind." But on July 6, 1885, an Alsatian mother brings her little boy, Joseph Meister, into Pasteur's laboratory. The boy is suffering intensely from fourteen bites inflicted by a mad dog two days earlier. The mother had taken her son at once to her local physician, but he could do nothing for her beyond cauterizing the wounds with carbolic acid. Must the boy die? Her physician had told her that her only hope was in Pasteur who knew more about this disease than anyone else, but who had never yet treated a human being afflicted with it. The mother now stands before Pasteur and implores him to save her son. He knows—no one better—the cost of failure: death for the boy, disgrace, possibly prison for himself, and certainly the end of his work in this field. Yet here are the pleading mother and the suffering boy. What to do?

He makes the mother and son as comfortable as possible in neighboring rooms, then hastens to secure the counsel of scientific friends. With their encouragement he decides to take the risk. He hurries back to the laboratory, selects a weak culture of the virus, and makes the first inoculation upon the boy. He follows this on succeeding days with inoculations of increasing strength. Each day he uses a more virulent culture.

"My dear children," writes his wife to their daughter and son, "your father had another bad night; he is dreading the last inoculation on the child. And yet there

176

can be no drawing back now. The boy continues in perfect health." The treatment lasts ten days during which Pasteur inoculates the lad twelve times. They are days of conflicting hopes and fears for the "mere chemist." After the last and most virulent injection, he sits by the boy's bedside watching his every movement. The child sleeps peacefully. Pasteur, weary and fearful, is sleepless, a prey to dark imaginings. . . . There is nothing further to do but wait. The days drag on—one, five, ten, twenty, thirty. The boy lives, completely cured! It is one of the great events in medical history.

Like the watch fires on the Grecian hills proclaiming the victory of Agamemnon and the fall of Troy, the news flashes across the world that Pasteur can cure hydrophobia. Afflicted men, women, and children, poor and rich, from France, England, Germany, Russia, and America begin their eager, fearful pilgrimage to his laboratory.

Pasteur Institute Established. To care for this increasing stream of sufferers some provision must be made. The little laboratory is soon taxed beyond its capacity. Thereupon the Academy of Sciences recommends that an establishment be created by popular subscription and known as the Pasteur Institute, its purpose to be the treatment of hydrophobia, research on other contagious and virulent diseases, and a center of teaching. Newspapers of many countries open their columns for subscriptions to this Institute. Millionaires, clerks, scrubwomen, and children gratefully offer their gifts. With swelling heart Pasteur reads the lengthening list of donors, and when, among the numerous subscriptions from Alsace, he notes the name of his first patient —little Joseph Meister—his eyes are brimming.

At the opening of the great building three years later, he is too moved to deliver the speech he has prepared and asks his son to read it for him. These extracts from it reveal the breadth and depth of the spirit of the man who, beginning as a humble tanner's son and as a slow but persevering pupil in the village school, has steadily forged ahead until he is among the outstanding scientists of the world and one of the greatest benefactors of humanity.

Keep your early enthusiasm, dear collaborators, but let it ever be regulated by rigorous examinations and tests. Never advance anything which cannot be proved in a simple and decisive fashion. . . .

It is indeed a hard task, when you believe you have found an important scientific fact and are feverishly anxious to publish it, to constrain yourself for days, weeks, years sometimes, to fight with yourself, to try to ruin your own experiments and only to proclaim your discovery after having exhausted all contrary hypotheses.

But when, after so many efforts, you have at last arrived at a certainty, your joy is one of the greatest which can be felt by a human soul. . . .

Two contrary laws seem to be wrestling with each other nowadays; the one, a law of blood and of death, ever imagining new means of destruction and forcing

178

nations to be constantly ready for the battlefield—the other, a law of peace, work, and health, ever evolving new means of delivering man from the scourges which beset him.

The one seeks violent conquests, the other the relief of humanity. The latter places one human life above any victory; while the former would sacrifice hundreds and thousands of lives to the ambition of one. The law of which we are the instruments seeks, even in the midst of carnage, to cure the sanguinary ills of the law of war; the treatment inspired by our antiseptic methods may preserve thousands of soldiers. Which of those two laws will ultimately prevail, God alone knows. But we may assert that French Science will have tried, by obeying the law of Humanity, to extend the frontiers of Life.

He is an old man, ill and weary, but his days are filled with the labor of directing this great Institute, and his mind with visions of further conquests in the "world of the infinitesimally small," where hundreds of diseases still lurk. One day he receives the following letter:

You have done all the good a man can do on earth. If you will, you can surely find a remedy for the horrible disease called diphtheria. Our children, to whom we teach your name as that of a great benefactor, will owe their lives to you.   A MOTHER.

Even before he receives this letter he is directing the work of two of his ablest assistants toward finding a cure for diphtheria. Other assistants are working on the bubonic plague. His former students, scattered throughout half a dozen countries, are applying his methods to still other diseases. Daily the mail brings him letters of their progress—reports of his young captains to their general in the war against mankind's deadly and invisible foes.

His Passing. In the midst of these activities, on November 1, 1894, Pasteur is stricken with a violent attack of uremia. Valiantly he struggles to fight off the inevitable end. But the years and his indefatigable labors have taken their toll of his strength. He grows weaker and weaker and paralysis creeps over his body. On September 28, 1895, in a room of almost monastic simplicity, surrounded by his family and his scientific friends, one hand clasping a crucifix, the other resting in that of his loving wife, very peacefully, he passes into the Great Unknown.

That last scene contains the essential elements for the understanding of the sources of power in Louis Pasteur—his family, his friends, his science, and his religious faith. From his earliest childhood he had been surrounded by the affections of a family whose mutual loyalty and self-sacrifice gave richness and beauty to life. His father, the old tanner, and his mother had taught him the dignity of labor, the virtue of honesty, and the grace of gratitude. His wife had watched over his health and his peace, shielding him from interruptions while he worked. His friends, selected with fine discrimination, had given him their encouragement, stood by him through his bitter struggles, restrained him when his enthusiasm would have led him away from the straight and narrow path of his researches. He, in turn, had shared their labors, taught them his methods, and given preference to them when honors were distributed.

And lastly, there was the crucifix. He had no superstitions, no fear of any devil that it might scare away. He clasped it because it represented the thing he counted of highest value—sacrificial love. Though he worshiped science, he never gave it the place of religion. Science bears no crosses. Only love knows how to bear a cross. Science at its best can give man knowledge, discoveries, inventions, cures. But science cannot give man motives, or goals, or courage, or hope, or the spirit of sacrifice. It cannot tame within the human heart the devils of greed and lust. He had seen science under the stress of war turn all its energies toward creating engines of human destruction. He had learned that something more than science is needed to make men want to help and not destroy each other. But let us listen to his own words on the subject:

There are two men in each of us: the scientist, he who starts with a clear field and desires to rise to the knowledge of Nature through observation, experimentation, and reasoning, and the man of sentiment, the man of belief, the man who mourns his dead children, and who cannot, alas, prove that he will see them again, but who believes that he will, and lives in that hope,

181

the man who will not die like a vibrio, but who feels that the force that is within man cannot die. The two domains are distinct, and woe to him who tries to let them trespass on each other in the so imperfect state of human knowledge.

With such a faith in his heart, he faced the unsolved problems of the universe with a humility as vast as it was genuine. It is not for us to judge, but Sir William Osler may have been right in declaring that Pasteur "was the most perfect man who has ever entered the Kingdom of Science."

BIBLIOGRAPHY

Thomas Jefferson

Adams, James Truslow: *The Living Jefferson*. Scribners. New York, 1936.

Bowers, Claude G.: *Jefferson and Hamilton*. Houghton Mifflin Company. Boston, 1925. Also *Jefferson in Power,* 1936.

Chinard, Gilbert: *Thomas Jefferson*. Little, Brown. Boston, 1929.

Beard, Charles A. and Mary R.: *The Rise of American Civilisation*. Macmillan. New York, 1927.

Hirst, Francis W.: *Life and Letters of Thomas Jefferson*. Macmillan. New York, 1926.

Jackson, Henry: *The Thomas Jefferson Bible..* Boni and Liveright. New York, 1923.

Jefferson, Thomas: *Autobiography*. Putnam, 1914.

Muzzey, David S.: *Thomas Jefferson*. Scribners, 1918.

Charles Dickens

A Collection of Letters of Dickens. Scribners. New York, 1889.

Chesterton, G. K.: *Charles Dickens: A Critical Study*. Dodd, Mead and Company. New York, 1906.

Crotch, W. W.: *Charles Dickens, Social Reformer*. Chapman & Hall, Ltd. London, 1913.

Fields, James T.: *Yesterdays with Authors*. Houghton Mifflin Company. Boston and New York, 1884.

Forster, John: *The Life of Charles Dickens*. J. B. Lippincott Company. Philadelphia, 1903.

Marzials, Frank T.: *Dickens*. Scribners. New York, 1887.

Dickens, Charles: *David Copperfield*. University Society. New York, 1908.

Dickens, Charles: *Old Curiosity Shop.* University Society. New York, 1908.

Matthew Arnold

(He wished that no formal life be written of himself.)
Works:
Culture and Anarchy. Macmillan, 1925.
Literature and Dogma. Macmillan, 1892.
Poems. Two volumes. Macmillan, 1877.
Letters. Two volumes. Edited by G. W. E. Russell. Macmillan. New York, 1896.
Discourses in America. Macmillan, 1889.
Sketches and Criticism:
Paul, Herbert W.: *Matthew Arnold.* Macmillan, 1925.
Russell, G. W. E.: *Matthew Arnold.* Scribners, 1904.

Louis Pasteur

Descour, L. (translated by A. F. Wedd): *Pasteur and His Work.* T. F. Unwin, Ltd. London, 1922.
Duclaux, E. (translated by E. F. Smith): *Pasteur: The History of a Mind.* W. B. Saunders Company. Philadelphia, 1920.
Vallery-Radot, René (translated from the French by Mrs. R. L. Devonshire): *The Life of Pasteur.* Garden City Publishing Company. Garden City, N. Y., 1926.

HOW TO RETAIN A BIOGRAPHY

If you read only for the enjoyment of the moment and want nothing more, this note is not for you. But if you want to retain what you have read and file it for future reference, you may find the following suggestion useful. Before you begin the reading of a biography jot down on a sheet of paper these headings:

1. *Heredity* (Chief characteristics of father, mother, and other forebears)
2. *Early Environment* (Nation and times, community, home, school, church, personalities)
3. *Later Environment* (Same in adult life)
4. *Purpose* (Note the various purposes by which the character steered his activities. Did he come finally to center his life around a single purpose? If so, what?)
5. *Opposition* (Who opposed him and why?)
6. *Handicaps* (Physical, social, economic)
7. *Achievements*
8. *Failures* (Vocational and personal)
9. *Sayings worth remembering*
10. *Dramatic scenes in his life*
11. *Religious beliefs or convictions*
12. *Personality* (Dominant moods and attitudes)

13. *Sources of his power* (Your own judgment
    here)
14. *Miscellany*

Then, as you read, make brief memoranda under these
headings, noting the page reference in each case. File
these notes along with those you make of other biographies. You will soon have an invaluable series of reference sources for public addresses, articles, or other educational uses.

I submitted the above outline—which is the one followed in the sketches in this volume—to the late
Gamaliel Bradford, dean of American biographers, ask-
ing for his suggestions upon it. In his reply he said,
"I am exceedingly interested in the questions in your
outline, for it is just precisely on that line that I have
been doing my own biographical work for the last
twenty years. More and more I am convinced of the
advantage of discarding the purely chronological
scheme and substituting as you do one that will bring
out psychological value and significance. Your syllabus
is admirably selected." On the strength of this endorse-
ment I am emboldened to pass on the outline to others.

F. E.